Helping College S
in Distress

MW01034535

This important resource draws from counseling and higher education professionals' insights to unpack real-life dilemmas of students in distress both inside and outside the classroom, while providing readers with essential tools and recommendations for assisting distressed students. The chapters in Part I examine the impact of emotional and mental health on the college campus, what college campuses are doing to address students' emotional and mental issues, the potential legal implications when dealing with students, and how faculty can and should approach this challenging topic. Each chapter in Part II includes a case narrative, along with a "Takeaways" section, which outlines and delineates the primary points faculty should consider when facing similar episodes involving distressed students. A "Questions for Reflection" section provides an opportunity for the reader to apply knowledge, reflect on their decision-making, and generate ideas individually or with peers. *Helping College Students in Distress* is a roadmap providing direction and examples of best practices for Higher Education faculty on the "front lines" in academia.

Monica Galloway Burke is a Professor of Counseling and Student Affairs at Western Kentucky University, USA.

Karl Laves is the Clinical Care Coordinator and Associate Director of the Counseling Center at Western Kentucky University, USA.

Jill Duba Sauerheber is a Professor and Department Head of Counseling and Student Affairs at Western Kentucky University, USA.

Aaron W. Hughey is a University Distinguished Professor of Counseling and Student Affairs and Coordinator of the Student Affairs graduate program at Western Kentucky University, USA.

Helping College Students in Distress

A Faculty Guide

Edited by
**Monica Galloway Burke,
Karl Laves,
Jill Duba Sauerheber, and
Aaron W. Hughey**

Routledge
Taylor & Francis Group

NEW YORK AND LONDON

First published 2021
by Routledge
52 Vanderbilt Avenue, New York, NY 10017

and by Routledge
2 Park Square, Milton Park, Abingdon, Oxon, OX14 4RN

Routledge is an imprint of the Taylor & Francis Group, an informa business

© 2021 Taylor & Francis

The right of Monica Galloway Burke, Karl Laves, Jill Duba Sauerheber, and Aaron W. Hughey to be identified as the authors of the editorial material, and of the authors for their individual chapters, has been asserted in accordance with sections 77 and 78 of the Copyright, Designs and Patents Act 1988.

All rights reserved. No part of this book may be reprinted or reproduced or utilized in any form or by any electronic, mechanical, or other means, now known or hereafter invented, including photocopying and recording, or in any information storage or retrieval system, without permission in writing from the publishers.

Trademark notice: Product or corporate names may be trademarks or registered trademarks, and are used only for identification and explanation without intent to infringe.

Library of Congress Cataloging-in-Publication Data
Names: Burke, Monica Galloway, editor. | Laves, Karl, editor. | Sauerheber, Jill Duba, editor. | Hughey, Aaron W., editor.
Title: Helping college students in distress : a faculty guide / edited by Monica Galloway Burke, Karl Laves, Jill Duba Sauerheber, Aaron W. ughey.
Identifiers: LCCN 2020013823 (print) | LCCN 2020013824 (ebook) | ISBN 9780367404628 (hardback) | ISBN 9780367416904 (paperback) | ISBN 9780367815738 (ebook)
Subjects: LCSH: Counseling in higher education–United States. | College students--Mental health–United States. | Stress in youth–United States.
Classification: LCC LB2343 .H36 2021 (print) | LCC LB2343 (ebook) | DDC 378.1/94–dc23
LC record available at https://lccn.loc.gov/2020013823
LC ebook record available at https://lccn.loc.gov/2020013824

ISBN: 978-0-367-40462-8 (hbk)
ISBN: 978-0-367-41690-4 (pbk)
ISBN: 978-0-367-81573-8 (ebk)

Typeset in Sabon
by Swales & Willis, Exeter, Devon, UK

Contents

CONTENTS

Preface

At the end of a workshop for faculty facilitated by Dr. Laves about responding to distressed students, a discussion developed with several faculty members who were sharing their experiences and asking what they could have done differently. As a result, Dr. Laves asked them if they would be interested in collecting stories and getting mental health practitioners and administrators to give responses and suggestions. The response was a resounding yes. Afterwards, he approached his fellow co-editors and shared the faculty's interest in a book that would provide recommendations and resources, and from there the idea for this book began.

As we converse and consult with faculty about student distress in higher education, we often hear confusion, frustration, uncertainty, as well as a commonality of occurrences. As student-centered higher education professionals and mental health practitioners and advocates, we believe that faculty should be provided content and tools to employ when a problem or question arises in working with a student in distress. Of course, there is a school of thought that endorses the idea that faculty should not be burdened or empowered to assist students with their mental health struggles. In doing so, some believe faculty are inadvertently set up to provide the "right" advice and direction to students in distress or crisis. Accompanying such arguments is the stance that reasonable efforts should be made to ensure that students are aware of the mental health services, but such efforts do not belong in the classroom or in the hands of faculty; but should reside with the professionals. Whether faculty believe they should not be burdened or expected to address their students' mental health challenges, some faculty will feel inclined to intervene when their students are experiencing distress inside or outside of the classroom.

We genuinely appreciate the courageous nature and trueness of our contributors who shared their stories and viewpoints. Discussing students in distress is a touchy subject and often not talked about openly. Being "exposed" and sharing with the public how they interacted with distressed students is bold and venerable. You will also notice that all of our contributors invested a great deal of self-reflection about how they intervened and helped distressed students. It is also worth mentioning that a book like this requires the use of actual student examples but also requires preventing a student being identified from the story. All efforts were made to obscure personal/descriptive information so that the student could not be identified.

The book is organized into 13 chapters. In Chapter 1, the editors provide an overview of topics related to helping students in distress and the topics that follow in the subsequent chapters, including the still evolving nature of faculty-student interactions, how college affects students and how mental health concerns impact the educational process, preliminary considerations when responding to students who are experiencing distress, an explanation of applicable terms and their definitions, and the theoretical framework that underpins successful interventions. Chapter 2 provides more in-depth information about the basic helping skills and competencies that should characterize an effective response to students in distress, including social interest, unconditional positive regard, relationship building, understanding and facilitating, relevant cultural considerations, and a brief guide for determining what to do and not do in any given situation.

In Chapter 3, Colin Cannonier, an Associate Professor of Economics at Belmont University, provides a narrative detailing an encounter he had with a student who exhibited multiple compounding factors and how he employed several strategies—involving the use of technology and consultation with colleagues—to deal with the immediate consequences as well as the more long-term implications for the student. In Chapter 4, Tonya Conston, a clinical assistant professor in the College of Education at the University of Houston, describes the impact traumatic personal loss can have on a student's educational pursuits and how empathy and getting a more complete picture of what is going on in a student's life are critical to helping them deal with life-changing events. In Chapter 5, Ryan Donovan, a Senior Teaching Instructor in the Department of Health and Exercise Science at Colorado State University, provides a narrative involving a student who was contemplating suicide. Included in the discussion are the limits of confidentiality when addressing these kinds of life-and-death situations, as well as the importance of consulting with mental health professionals who can provide much-needed insights and recommendations.

In Chapter 6, Christopher L. Giroir, an Associate Professor in Educational Leadership at the University of Louisiana at Lafayette, discusses the challenges he had attempting to deal with an older student who was disruptive and had an exceptionally distressing influence on the other students in the class, including the importance of understanding cross-generational dynamics and how to cope with a lack of administrative support. In Chapter 7, Lia Howard, an Assistant Professor of Political Science and Liberal Studies at Eastern University, provides two encounters she had with students who were experiencing significant life changes/transitions—one involving intra-familial conflict related to pregnancy/abortion and one involving a male who was transitioning to a female. These situations illustrate the complexity of intervening when the cause of student distress has moral and cultural dimensions.

In Chapter 8, Trish Lindsey Jaggers, an Assistant Professor in the Department of English at Western Kentucky University, addresses how to deal with the angst that often surfaces when a student is struggling with identity issues, especially when those issues are in conflict with familial, religious and cultural beliefs, and mores. In Chapter 9, Dr. Andrea Kirk-Jenkins, an Assistant Professor in the Department of Counseling and Student Affairs at Western Kentucky University, describes the conflict that often materializes when the immediate emotional and physical needs of an individual student supersede the needs of the other students in the class. These situations, which also involve self-care, are often impossible to resolve without the assistance of colleagues and other supportive individuals.

In Chapter 10, Dr. Theresia Johnson-Ratliff, Director of Field Education in the School of Social Work at Jackson State University, details what can happen—and what to do—when the topic of discussion in the classroom or individual meetings can trigger unpleasant memories and feelings for students. Specifically, involvement in an abusive relationship can precipitate complex, traumatic and hard to predict reactions from both traditional and nontraditional students. In Chapter 11, Dr. Leigh Johnson-Migalski, an Associate Professor in the Department of Psychology at Adler University, describes her encounter with a potentially suicidal student. Included in the narrative are not only her efforts to deal directly with the immediate needs of the student involved, but also her ancillary professional responsibilities and obligations when a student indicates that they may be contemplating ending their own life.

In Chapter 12, Megan X. Schutte, an Associate Professor of English at the Community College of Baltimore County, details her involvement with a student who experienced a cascade of unfortunate events within a relatively short amount of time (infidelity, homelessness, financial insecurity). The importance of helping the student appropriately without feeling the need to "rescue" them is explored. In Chapter 13, Dr. Sylvia Mendoza Aviña, a Lecturer in the Department of Bicultural-Bilingual Studies at the University of Texas at San Antonio, describes how a situation can evolve that entails a large group of distressed students, especially when cultural and individual identities, the intersection of societal and political circumstances, and generational and hegemonic beliefs become intertwined. As noted, these potentially volatile encounters must be negotiated sensitively yet definitively.

Our purpose is to provide a framework and a roadmap, not a paint-by-numbers, cookie-cutter approach. As such, each narrative concludes with a "Takeaways" section, which outlines and delineates the primary points faculty should consider when facing similar episodes involving distressed students, and a "Questions for Reflection" section, which contains several thought-provoking queries that faculty can reflect upon, either individually or with colleagues, in order to clarify the issues and approaches outlined in the respective narratives. The editors included a "Takeaway" to each narrative so that the reader can review the main points related to assisting a student or students in distress and use this knowledge to formulate strategies to aid in the helping process. The "Questions for Reflection" for each narrative provides an opportunity for the reader to apply knowledge and thoughts, reflect on their decision-making, and generate ideas individually or with peers. Keep in mind that every encounter with a distressed student (or students) is unique and includes its own set of inimitable circumstances. At the same time, there are clearly established principles and guidelines that have proven utility when addressing students who are exhibiting and experiencing distress. It is our hope that this book will provide direction and examples of best practices in addressing and working with students who are in distress.

Part I

The Framework and Roadmap

Chapter One

Faculty Helping Students in Distress

Monica Galloway Burke, Karl Laves, Jill Duba Sauerheber, and Aaron W. Hughey

> Amber has spent most of her life taking care of others and overcoming obstacles. Although she has moved 60 miles from home for college, her parents still expect her to contribute to the household income as she did in high school and care for her younger siblings when they need her to help. Amber has intermittently been taking medication since high school to help with her bouts of depression or her anxiety, or both simultaneously. Her first semester of college was very difficult, not because of the academic performance and expectations, but because she found it difficult to balance helping her family with her academics. One day, Amber walks into the department's office suite where several faculty members are congregated and when one asks her about her day thus far, she responds with a somber tone and solemn expression, "at least I have not thrown myself in front of a bus today; so, there's that."

If you were in the group with the faculty who had just heard Amber's response, what would you think? What would you say? What would you do? Would you perceive that her response indicated intent or distress? Was it just a flippant remark? Uncertainty in this type of situation is a natural reaction.

As you are probably aware, faculty can often encounter very distressed students who do not have "simple" problems like test anxiety or homesickness and the encounter can even occur unexpectedly. However, when they do happen, these encounters typically require quite a degree of focus, intentionality, and priority. Since these events typically come as a surprise, faculty are expected to respond promptly and often without preparation. Therefore, conversations about helping distressed students and the preparation to work with distressed students need to come before the event.

As a faculty member, have you ever had to experience the following?

- A student is belligerent or angry toward you in your office or in the classroom.
- A student discussion becomes a heated argument with threats.
- A student reveals to you that they are having thoughts of suicide.
- A student reveals to you that they have been sexually assaulted, are being stalked, or being harassed.
- A student tells you they have experienced racist and/or sexist remarks from others on campus.
- A student is experiencing discrimination because of their gender/ sexual identity and expression.
- A student tells you they are depressed and have difficulty getting out of bed each day.
- A student exhibits a great deal of neediness and dependency or there is a lack of boundaries.
- A student requests an excessive number of meetings, shows up often, and you have difficulty ending meetings with them.

Such interactions can leave any of us troubled and wondering how to respond. For people who are not trained to be helping professionals, the thought of figuring out what to do can be even more challenging. What would you say, if anything? With whom should you consult? What approach should be taken? Should you respond at all?

Faculty are trained to disseminate content knowledge and once in their faculty role they soon must develop a teaching style and methods, evaluate student performance based on learning outcomes, manage the classroom environment, stay informed in order to respond to student queries, and advise them appropriately. However, in addition to these responsibilities, faculty can find themselves dealing with issues for which they may feel unprepared, including responding to a student's emotional need, resolving interpersonal conflicts, facilitating mediations, and consulting with others to meet students' needs.

For example, in 2012, a 24-year-old student at Florida Atlantic University, who had been diagnosed with bipolar disorder since the age of 13 and sub-sequently diagnosed with schizophrenia, had an outburst in a classroom while the instructor was teaching. The incident, which was videotaped by several students in the class, included her screaming and cursing, threatening her peers and the professor, as well as striking a male classmate in the head. As her behavior began to escalate, the professor continued to stand in front of the classroom, attempting to teach and respond to a question she asked. A couple of minutes passed, and another faculty member entered the classroom to intervene. He began yelling at and arguing with the student and insisted that she leave the classroom. The visiting faculty member and the student eventually ended up in a brief scuffle. The FAU police soon arrived and took the student to South County Mental Health Center, reportedly tasering her three times in the process. The student was Baker Acted (involuntary admission due to mental breakdown) for the third time in her life. The student's mother and sister reported that this incident was not the first time she had an outburst due to her mental illness. The family also reported that she is usually very shy and reserved; however, around the time of this incident she had just started taking a new medication. The family thinks the professor should have realized that something was wrong and should have reacted differently. The professor indicated that he realized there was a mental health issue, which is why he did not confront her, and his Teaching Assistant had left the classroom to call the police (see Chapnick, 2012).

Based on the above description of the incident, we can gather a few facts. First, the faculty member had to deal with an unexpected student in distress, which of course impacted the rest of the class. Second, many of the students remained in the classroom during the incident, which was not necessarily in the best interest of their safety. Third, another instructor entered the classroom and intervened without being fully aware of the circumstances instead of waiting for law enforcement. There are remaining pieces of information that were not apparent but could have likely prevented the incident from developing into what it did. Was the instructor of the course informed and trained in dealing with such difficult and disruptive situations in the classroom? During the incident, were the engaging faculty members considering what the consequences of their actions or inaction would be, as well as how the crisis was impacting their ability to provide a productive and safe learning environment?

In observing such incidents, note that it is not the psychological issue or diagnosis itself that is significant, but how such issues may influence the student and their micro (classroom) and macro (i.e., academic, residential, and social) community. If the student's behavior or performance is not a problem, the diagnosis or mental health history is not necessarily relevant. However, if a student's mental health appears to be influencing their behavior or performance and puts the student, their peers, and the instructor in a precarious position, then the faculty should address it. Of course, there is not a fool-proof, cookie-cutter approach to working with students in distress; however, there are considerations and basic helping skills that can be used in the process.

Since faculty interact with students often, they may be the first person a student seeks out for help when distressed and are in a position to notice if a student is exhibiting concerning behavior. Since a safe learning

5

environment is a necessity for a successful academic environment, all involved must feel safe and supported. Faculty can also serve an influential role because not only can they provide reassurance, they can also be a link to resources for a student in mental or emotional distress. Without appropriate resources and skillsets, faculty in a position to help a student in distress may often employ a reactive approach. Reactive approaches are important because an actual response occurs; but waiting for students to be fully engaged in their distress and exhibit alarming behavior before showing concern or offering support may not be the most effective way to address their mental well-being. Should faculty prepare for discussions with students about the amount of stress and feelings they may be experiencing and reactions as they struggle in that moment? As such, faculty should be proactive in preparing and taking positive steps in advance toward anticipating the unexpected rather than waiting for something to occur and then reacting when students come to them in distress. As the saying goes, expect the best, plan for the worst, and prepare to be surprised.

This book introduces narratives composed by college faculty sharing real-life situations with students in distress inside and outside of the college classroom and how they responded. First, we begin by discussing the impact of emotional and mental health, distress, and related issues on the college campus. Next, we explain what college campuses are doing to address students' emotional and mental issues and the potential legal implications when dealing with students who are experiencing emotional distress. Essential tools to effectively assist college students include understanding the warning signs for mental health problems of college students; distinguishing what signs indicate emotional distress; and knowing whom to contact if signs are there and if there are questions or concerns about a student's behavior. As such, we then discuss the role of faculty and expectations when helping students in distress and how faculty can use basic helping skills in facilitating the process. Finally, the book provides actual situations told from the viewpoint of faculty in which they have been confronted with students who are experiencing emotional and mental distress. Each narrative is followed with information, considerations, and questions for reflection related to engaging with students in a psychologically present manner and how faculty can choose behaviors to get the student to the appropriate service provider if necessary.

THE IMPACT OF MENTAL HEALTH

Mental health is a core component essential for all humans' overall health and functioning. When our mental health is in a good state, we manage our basic cognitive and social skills; recognize, express, and modulate our emotions; are flexible and able to cope with adverse life events; function in social roles; and modulate a harmonious relationship between our body and mind (Galderisi, Heinz, Kastrup, Beezhold, & Sartorius, 2015). However, when we experience diminished capacities—cognitive, emotional, attentional, interpersonal, motivational, or behavioral—our enjoyment of life or interactions with society and the environment can be adversely affected (Stephens, Dulberg, & Joubert, 1999). A basic assumption is that people pursue pleasant emotions and avoid unpleasant ones. Of course, no one feels their best when experiencing unhappiness, relationship problems, and a lack of motivation or focus as we live our life roles and interact with our environments.

At its most basic level, college is an environment filled with interactions, introspection, discovery, choices, conflicts, and judgment. For college students, college life is also filled with new opportunities to grow and learn. As we grow and learn in life, anxiety, fear, worry, disappointment, sadness, and anger are as much a part of it as joy, passion, curiosity, delight, and contentment, which often involve unpleasant as well as pleasant emotions. Experiencing unpleasant situations can impact a variety of aspects of a college student's life such as academics, interpersonal relationships, physical well-being, emotional health, work life, and family dynamics. In these contexts, it is not uncommon for a student to experience distress or mental health issues.

MENTAL HEALTH ISSUES ON THE COLLEGE CAMPUS

The number of college students who seek counseling for mental and emotional concerns has increased in recent years. An American Freshman Survey (Eagan et al., 2014) concluded that the emotional health of incoming freshmen is at its lowest point in at least three decades. Additionally, in the Association for University and College Counseling Center Directors (AUCCCD) annual survey of counseling center directors, a majority of the directors reported that the severity of student mental health concerns and related behavior on their campuses have risen (Reetz, Bershad, LeViness, & Whitlock, 2016). Common mental health issues reported by American college students include depression, stress, anxiety, and suicidal ideation in addition to concerns about feeling lonely and overwhelmed, relationships, family, and interpersonal functioning (Brandy, Penckofer, Solari-Twadell, & Velsor-Friedrich, 2015; LeViness, Bershad, & Gorman, 2017).

To establish clarity and common understanding with the subsequent content related to mental and emotional health, definitions of terms and concepts associated with this chapter follow.

7

Anxiety is defined as an emotion characterized by feelings of tension, worry, and physical changes (Kazdin, 2000). It has also been defined as a vague, uncomfortable feeling exacerbated by prolonged stress and the presence of multiple stressors (Lazarus & Folkman, 1984). In a typical reaction to stressful situations, anxiety can affect a person behaviorally (e.g., indecisive about answers, find it difficult to organize thoughts, difficulty with recall/going blank), cognitively (e.g., nervousness and low confidence), and physiologically (e.g., panic, perspiration, and muscle tension).

Depression is a negative affective state, ranging from unhappiness and discontent to an extreme feeling of sadness, pessimism, and despondency, that interferes with daily life with various physical, cognitive, and social changes that tend to co-occur (*APA Dictionary of Psychology*, n.d.). Symptoms of depression include altered eating or sleeping habits, lack of energy or motivation, difficulty concentrating or making decisions, withdrawal from social activities once enjoyed, feelings of hopelessness or worthlessness almost every day, restlessness, and weight gain or loss. It is different from the mood variations and sadness (although sadness is a symptom of depression) that people regularly experience as a part of life. Depression consists of episodes during which multiple symptoms last for at least two weeks.

Distress, also referred to as **psychological distress or mental distress**, is a negative stress response, often involving negative affect and physiological reactivity, that results from being overwhelmed by demands, losses, or perceived threats (*APA Dictionary of Psychology*, n.d.). It is viewed as an emotional disturbance that may impact the social functioning and day-to-day living of individuals (Wheaton, 2007). Psychological distress is also generally described as a state of emotional suffering characterized by symptoms of depression (e.g., lost interest, sadness, and hopelessness) and anxiety (e.g., restlessness and feeling tense) (Mirowsky & Ross, 2002). Distress varies among individuals and is not necessarily an illness (Peake & Mullings, 2016).

Mental health is "a state of well-being in which the individual realizes his or her own abilities, can cope with the normal stresses of life, can work productively and fruitfully, and is able to make a contribution to his or her community" (World Health Organization, 2018). It includes our emotional, psychological, and social well-being and affects how we think, feel, and act. It also helps determine how we handle stress, relate to others, and make choices.

Mental health illnesses are health conditions involving changes in emotion, thoughts, or behavior (or a combination of these) that comprise a broad range of problems, with different symptoms. Mental illnesses are associated with distress and/or problems functioning in social, work, or family activities (American Psychological Association, n.d.). Mental illnesses take many forms from mild, which only interfere in limited ways with daily life, or so severe that a person may need care in a hospital. A similarly related term is **mental health disorders**.

Microaggressions are "brief and commonplace daily verbal, behavioral and environmental indignities, whether intentional or unintentional, that communicate hostile, derogatory, or negative racial slights and insults to the target person or group" (Sue et al., 2007, p. 273). Microaggressions can cause students to experience serious cognitive, behavioral, and emotional reactions, making it very difficult for them to learn (Sue, Lin, Torino, Capodilupo, & Rivera, 2009).

Stress is "a highly personalized phenomenon that varies between people depending on individual vulnerability and resilience, and between different types of tasks" (Fink, 2016, p. 3). Stress occurs when environmental demands exceed an individual's perception of their ability to cope.

Suicidal ideation is thinking about serving as the agent for one's own death, ranging in seriousness depending on the specificity of suicide plans and the degree of suicidal intent—from fleeting thoughts, to extensive thoughts, to detailed planning (American Psychological Association, 2010). Suicidal ideations may vary in seriousness depending on the specificity of suicide plans and the degree of suicidal intent. Suicidal ideations can be passive, which implies a desire to die without a specific plan (e.g., a wish to die during sleep, to be killed in an accident, or to develop terminal cancer) or active, which is an existing desire to die with a specific plan for their death (Barry, Wakefield, Trestman, & Conwell, 2016). A closely related term is **suicidality**.

The Changes that College Can Bring

The college experience offers multiple opportunities for personal and professional development. Students may for the first time experience the freedom in making choices about relationships, finances, future planning, and how to manage academics balanced with enjoyment. The freedom, independence, and opportunity to engage in new and different experiences also can be accompanied by stress. Depending on multiple internal (i.e., predispositions including biopsychosocial predispositions, and current states), as well as external (i.e., health of support systems, resources) factors, these experiences can become stressors that place college students at a greater risk for anxiety, depression, and other mental and emotional challenges. Of course, most college students experience stress, but when stress becomes distress they are at risk of decreased academic performance, academic attrition, and depression (Kadison & Digeronimo, 2004; Melnyk et al., 2015).

9

As the Yerkes-Dodson law (1908) purports, a certain level of stress is necessary and results in optimal performance, but only up to a point. If the level of stress becomes too high, performance decreases and if the source of stress is perceived as insignificant or, more likely, as exceeding the capacity to cope, then distress ensues. For example, during an exam, if a person's anxiety level is at an optimal level (they are mentally aroused), the alertness could help them remember content to answer questions; but if they are experiencing too much stress, the person's ability to focus and recall information could be hampered. The optimal level of stress is also referred to as eustress (Lazarus, 1974), which is defined as a positive stress response that involves an optimal level of stimulation and results from challenging but attainable tasks (*APA Dictionary of Psychology*, n.d.).

Too much stress can lead to health problems and stressors that can influence mood, sense of well-being, behavior, and health (Schneiderman, Ironson, & Siegel, 2005). Distress has been described as the sum of exposure and vulnerability divided by the sum of psychological resources and social support and, as such, a stressor alone will not predict the level of distress in a student; therefore, the student's vulnerabilities, psychological resources, and amount of social support must be known (Burke, Sauerheber, Hughey, & Laves, 2017). This model and equation are described in detail in Vitaliano, Maiuro, Bolton, and Armsden (1987). Their model is shown in the equation below.

$$distress = \frac{exposure\ to\ stressors + vulnerability}{psychological\ and\ social\ resources}$$

Our perceptions are molded and shaped by previous experiences and how we have made sense of those experiences. Through these experiences, we oftentimes encounter stressors. Briefly, stressors are life events that may be perceived as demanding or threatening, requiring the person to exert more effort or energy to respond. Stressors fall into three categories based on severity: hassles, major life events, and catastrophic events. Hassles are minor, perhaps daily, events that can be stressful but by themselves are not overwhelming. Major life events are more significant and while many are normal and a part of the life cycle (i.e., giving birth, death, illness, marriage, divorce, loss of a relationship), they can still cause disruption and often major adaptation. The events are within the realm of the expected, but, depending on whether they are expected or wanted, they can be stressful. Catastrophes are events that are beyond what would be expected in a typical lifetime. Assaults, natural disasters, and war are examples of catastrophic events that one would not expect to experience and can be overwhelming.

Vulnerabilities are experiences or qualities of a person that make a stressor more demanding. Vulnerabilities are not chosen by a person; they are acquired and/or developmental in nature, which include external as well as internal factors. External (outside of the individual) would include growing up in poverty, childhood abuse, and oppression/marginalization. For example, a first-generation student may have a harder time coping with a normal college stressor because of a lack of information about college life. Internal, or organic vulnerabilities, might include a predisposition to stress, chemical (hormonal) imbalances, over- or under-active autonomic nervous system, as well as chronic illness. Vulnerabilities may be thought of as the cards that life deals you. The game is less stressful if you start off with good cards.

Psychological and social resources can amend (in the positive or negative) our experiences with stress and our vulnerabilities. Psychological resources, for example, are attitudes, skills, and dispositions we are taught and modeled by our attachment figures and other mature adults. They are philosophies, theologies, and perspectives that provide hope, patience, and encouragement. They are also skills that can be learned along the way like relaxation, mindfulness, asking for help, and tolerating anxiety. Social resources are, essentially, the people with whom we have relationships (e.g., a best friend, sibling, or life partner) or they can be found in the groups we belong to or are affiliated with (e.g., sorority, church, community). Having supportive family, friends, and acquaintances, as well as having relationship skills to find and maintain supportive people, can also help buffer the effects of a stressor and vulnerabilities. You will note that it is not the event or the stressor that directly causes distress.

CONSIDERATIONS FOR INSTITUTIONS OF HIGHER EDUCATION WHEN RESPONDING TO STUDENTS IN DISTRESS

Since the goal of higher education is to assist students with their matriculation to graduation, addressing mental health issues cannot be overlooked. Students experiencing mental health problems can be profoundly affected physically, emotionally, and cognitively, which can impact the individual, interpersonal, and institutional levels of a college campus, including academic progress, retention, and graduation rates (Arria et al., 2013; Eisenberg, Golberstein, & Hunt, 2009; Kitzrow, 2003). For example, the National College Health Assessment (American College Health Association, 2018) reported that about one-third (33.2%) of college students identified stress as a factor and primary cause for impaired academic performance at some point in the previous year in addition to anxiety (26.5%).

11

Understanding a student's level of distress is important because when students are physically and emotionally drained, they can be affected within and beyond the classroom (e.g., academic success and social relationships). Since retention is a primary goal of higher education, professionals in higher education should recognize when they need to respond to students in distress and, if necessary, recommend professional counseling. In a survey of counseling directors (AUCCCD), of the students asked whether counseling services helped with their academic performance, 66.8% responded that counseling services had a positive impact on their academic performance and 65.2% reported that counseling services helped them stay in school (LeViness et al., 2017). However, as much as we want to promote student success, there are times when withdrawing from the university can be a good strategy for a student in distress. Some students would do well to sit out a semester, commit to therapy, access better health care and come back stronger a semester later.

An important consideration when dealing with students who are experiencing mental and emotional challenges involves the manner in which the institution responds to the students involved as well as those who are affected by their actions (Miller & Sorochty, 2015). Professionals charged with dealing with these kinds of situations should be well-versed in their respective roles and fully aware of the policies and procedures that are to be employed when unfortunate circumstances arise (Wilson, 2007). There is a myriad of dimensions that must be addressed when mounting an effective response (i.e., each dimension should address not only the students involved, but also minimize the potential harm to the campus community).

First, an institution should have protocols in place to deal with students who are experiencing mental and emotional distress before a situation evolves (Sharkin, 2010). Next, everyone at the institution should be fully aware of what to do when responding to these kinds of adverse situations. Moreover, the response needs to be coordinated in that everyone should be on the same page with respect to what should be done and who should be doing it (Zdziarski, Rollo, & Dunkel, 2007). As such, a collective understanding of the types of situations that could potentially arise should be determined, together with a similar understanding of how these situations should be addressed while considering the reality of the environment.

The institutional response to students experiencing emotional distress should be coordinated, evidence-based, and consistent (Sharkin, 2010). Therefore, the orientation of new employees from all sectors of the campus community (faculty, staff, administrators, and graduate assistants) should include information about the proper policies and procedures for engaging in an effective response. Further, this information should be a part of all ongoing professional development activities sponsored by the institution and the topic should receive regular attention at departmental and unit meetings throughout the academic year (Alexander & Alexander, 2017). These efforts should include and take into consideration the fact that there is no "one" correct way of dealing with students in distress as people have different styles, capacities, abilities, and limits, as well as knowing when to refer and how to consult (Amanda, 2015).

When dealing with distressed students, there are basically three levels of behavior that serve as indicators of what an adequate response should entail. Level 1 behaviors are those that are not disruptive but suggest a need for some assistance—i.e., serious grade problems and/or unaccountable changes in academic performance, attendance problems, marked changes in mood, activity or speech, changes in physical appearance, or difficulties staying conscious during class (Iarovici, 2014). With Level 1 behaviors, the student is not in any imminent danger, but there is a cause for concern and an intervention is warranted to prevent further deterioration.

Level 2 behaviors indicate that the student is experiencing significant emotional distress, often accompanied by a reluctance or even an inability to acknowledge or request help. These behaviors include repeated requests for special consideration; new or consistently occurring behaviors that are inherently unsettling and pushes limits; and an unusual or exaggerated emotional response that is disproportionate to the cause of the response (Benton & Benton, 2006).

Level 3 behaviors are the most critical as they often involve life or death consequences. When a student exhibits these behaviors, an immediate and purposeful response is necessary—e.g., highly disruptive behaviors (overt hostility often combined with aggression), inability to communicate clearly, a loss of contact with reality, overt suicidal thoughts, and homicidal threats (Fox & Burstein, 2010).

Again, the first step in formulating an effective institutional response to students in emotional distress involves appropriately identifying the category of the behavior exhibited (Degges-White & Borzumato-Gainey, 2013). As such, all faculty, staff, and administrators should be thoroughly trained on how to recognize the different behavioral levels and what course of action to initiate with each. All should know that their role is only to screen for behaviors—not diagnose. Only appropriately credentialed mental health professionals are able to engage in the diagnosis process.

In general, in order to respond effectively to students who are experiencing emotional distress, everyone at the institution should be able to (a) recognize basic symptomology, (b) make an appropriate referral, and (c) consult with mental health and other helping professionals

13

(Reynolds, 2009). Fundamentally, the first step in responding to distressed students is to make sure all faculty, staff, and administrators are endowed with the skill sets associated with these three procedures (McClellan & Stringer, 2009).

A Campus System of Support

One of the most effective strategies for being proactive when it comes to effectively responding to students who are exhibiting emotional distress involves the use of a Behavioral Intervention Team (BIT) (Sokolow & Lewis, 2016). Although these formal committees often go by different names (e.g., threat assessment team, student crisis action team, etc.), their mission is always the same—to identify and monitor students who have the potential to disrupt the campus environment by doing harm to themselves or others (Hunt & Eisenberg, 2010; National Association of School Psychologists, 2015). They are typically comprised of representatives from all constituencies of the campus (faculty, staff, administrators, student affairs professionals) and they meet periodically to discuss students who have been identified as being potentially capable of engaging in counterproductive behaviors (Hansen & Diliberti, 2019; Sokolow & Lewis, 2016). Their meetings are typically closed, and their discussions are considered highly confidential. Anyone on campus can report students who are engaging in questionable behaviors to the behavioral intervention team and then the group decides on the best course of action (National Association of School Psychologists, 2015).

Legal Implications

Finally, everyone at the institution should be cognizant of the potential legal implications of their actions when dealing with students who are experiencing emotional distress (Alexander & Alexander, 2017). For instance, The Family Educational Rights and Privacy Act (FERPA) protects the privacy of student education records at all schools that receive funds under an applicable program of the U.S. Department of Education, prohibiting higher education institutions from sharing information in student records with parents, with narrow exceptions such as in a health or safety emergency. However, FERPA does not prohibit the sharing of information regarding personal observations and other knowledge about a particular student with other campus officials, especially when there is a legitimate safety concern such as when the professional feels the student may be a danger to themselves or others (Ramirez, 2009). For example, concerns about safety that warrant disclosure could include a student's suicidal statements or ideations, erratic, angry, or threatening behaviors, or similar conduct that others would reasonably see as posing a risk of serious harm to the student or others. Note that FERPA governs records only, not information obtained through personal knowledge, observations, or data (U.S. Department of Education, 2011). If you are unsure if disclosure is necessary to protect the health and safety of the student, seek consultation from the Counseling Center, Student Conduct Office, or your campus counsel. Furthermore, if a parent contacts you for information, you can listen to their concerns and let them know you will get back to them after you get clarity on what information you can release. In addition, inform them of the protections within FERPA.

Similarly, everyone should be aware of the Americans with Disabilities Act (ADA) and its implications for students who are experiencing emotional distress (Jordan, 1996; U.S. Department of Labor, 2019). Students with emotional and mental health conditions are increasingly subject to the protections afforded under the ADA and related legislation as these conditions, especially when diagnosed, can be classified as a disability (Huger, 2011). You cannot make decisions or act in any way that shows bias toward or discriminate against someone with a mental health difficulty or history.

In short, institutions of higher education should have developed protocols related to meeting the challenges associated with students experiencing mental and emotional challenges, as well as having adequate services and resources to support them. Although those who work in student services are often educated and trained to identify signs of concern and work with students who are emotionally and mentally distressed, faculty for the most part would have to learn by trial and error and lean on their natural abilities to help others. Institutions are behooved to provide training or at least have ample resources for faculty.

FACULTY ROLES AND EXPECTATIONS WHEN HELPING STUDENTS IN DISTRESS

A common query posed by faculty is about how to differentiate between a student who may have a mental health disorder/issue or who is just exhibiting disruptive behavior, followed by a request for suggestions on how to respond to a student who is disruptive but also seems to be in distress. Of course, it could oftentimes be difficult to distinguish since symptoms of distress are present in both situations. It would also be hard to know the origin or motive for disruptive behavior without talking to the student. In some cases, the disruptive behavior might be attributed to a disorder based on observation (e.g., if the student is having a psychotic episode or a panic attack).

Many faculty feel they should not be expected to handle disruptive behavior from a student conduct perspective if the student has a psychological disorder. But, generally speaking, faculty are encouraged to first address the behavior and then see if the student will share that they have a diagnosed disorder. However, an angry outburst in class is not excused behavior because the student has been diagnosed as being on the spectrum, depressed, or phobic. After addressing the behavior, the student can be encouraged to seek counseling if they feel it would help.

It should be noted that an isolated disruption does not necessitate the involvement of the university's student conduct office. It simply may mean that the behavior needs to be addressed with the student so that it does not continue. If the issue can be resolved between the faculty member and the student, a report to the student conduct office is not typically warranted. When the student continues the disruptive behavior or does not seem to understand why the behavior is disruptive, then contacting the student conduct office or the Dean of Students is justified. Ultimately, disruptive behavior should not be excused as all students must abide by the code of conduct at an institution of higher education. However, faculty are encouraged to look for reasons and adapt their responses to the student based on what they know about the student's motives and needs.

Again, speaking in general terms, the difference between being disruptive due to a disorder and being disruptive due to personality is often not clear; but students with diagnosed disorders (e.g., depression and anxiety) tend to be apologetic, embarrassed, and are usually open to having a private conversation with faculty. However, students with anti-social, histrionic, or narcissistic personalities tend to blame their environment for their outbursts. Some students are, simply put, spoiled or entitled, and are more likely to engage in disruptive or attention-seeking behavior. Students on the spectrum might have trouble with editing their comments, interrupting discussions, but, for example, are usually open to having a private discussion to discuss what they need and how to conduct themselves. Essentially, there are multiple factors that will be unique to each and every student you encounter.

Recognizing Distress and When to Act

Identifying students who are emotionally distressed is often relatively straightforward, although it is always possible to misread the potential indicators and students tend to exhibit characteristics in different ways (Sharkin, 2011). Knowing how to intervene when a student has been correctly identified as experiencing emotional distress is a more challenging proposition for a number of reasons related to the continuing evolution of the college student population (Reynolds, 2009). Nonetheless, sensing distress can be intuitive. Faculty can take the opportunity and ask students about their distress. Answers to these inquisitive questions can help guide faculty towards which next steps are the most appropriate.

Also, in recognizing students in distress, observation is key. In looking for signs of distress in students, there are behaviors and circumstances to note that could be a reason to be concerned. Table 1.1 below, although not exhaustive, lists some of these signs.

Table 1.1 Signs of Distress.

Emotional and Cognitive	■ Feels very sad or is withdrawn for more than two weeks (can include regular crying, feeling fatigued, and unmotivated) ■ Acknowledges experiencing stress, anxiety, and panic attacks ■ Exhibits a variety of negative emotions ■ Exhibits irrational behavior, lack of judgment, irritability ■ Expresses suicidal thoughts and hopelessness and/or threats to self-harm ■ Expresses homicidal thoughts ■ Makes statements that are disconnected from reality
Addictive-like and Risk-taking Behaviors	■ Problematic internet use ■ Excessive use of social media (e.g., Facebook, Instagram) and/or smartphone ■ Excessive drinking or use of drugs ■ Consistency in gambling ■ Extreme risk-taking behaviors
Communication	■ Odd behavior and speech patterns ■ Impaired speech or garbled and disjointed thoughts ■ Bizarre behavior, speech, writing, or thinking ■ Engages in angry or hostile outbursts, yelling, or aggressive comments
Academic	■ Decreased concentration, motivation, and interest ■ Procrastination and poorly prepared work ■ Several missed assignments, exams, or appointments ■ Infrequent class attendance ■ Falling asleep in class ■ Extreme disorganization or erratic performance ■ Written or creative expression consisting of unusual violence, morbidity, social isolation, despair or confusion, or focus on suicide or death ■ Continual seeking of special provisions (extensions on assignments or deadlines, request extra credit or make-up exams) ■ Patterns of perfectionism: e.g., can't accept themselves if they do not get a very high grade/score ■ Overblown or disproportionate response to grades or other evaluations

(Continued)

17

Table 1.1 (*Continued*)

Social	■ Isolation and withdrawal
	■ Relationship distress
	■ Friends/peers may report something
	■ Rejection
Physical	■ Self-harm (i.e., cutting, wearing long sleeves on a blistering hot day)
	■ Poor personal hygiene
	■ Lethargic looking
	■ Visible changes in weight gain/loss
	■ Sleep gain/loss or insomnia
	■ Shakiness, tremors, fidgeting or pacing
	■ Disorganized speech, recognizable confusion
	■ Infrequent inability to make eye contact
	■ Attends class smelling of alcohol or other substances
Faculty–Student Relationship Dynamics	■ Neediness and dependency
	■ Lack of boundaries
	■ Excessive disclosure and/or problem-solving about personal issues and crises
	■ Unreasonable requests
	■ Excessive number of meetings
	■ Difficulty ending meetings
	■ Students showing up often
	■ Spending much of their spare time visiting during office hours or at other times

Everyone who may have to deal with students exhibiting signs of distress should also be aware of key cultural and socioeconomic factors and their relation to how behaviors are manifested in various populations (Sharkin, 2011). Students from underrepresented populations, for example, tend to exhibit different behaviors when they are distressed as compared to students who are not. Racism, sexism, homophobia, disability status, and gender identification can also present barriers for certain students in their quest to find assistance for what they are experiencing (Rutherford, 2010). Therefore, cultural considerations must always be taken into account when working with students from marginalized groups.

Now that the indicators of distress have been outlined, the next topic to consider is ways to respond when students are in distress. Based on your observation and categorization of the student's behavior, you will then determine an action. When you notice a sign or signs that a student is in distress and there is not an immediate risk of harm, a simple conversation with the student to obtain a better sense of their current situation would work best. You can even offer resources to a student. However, if there are signs that the student's behavior may be deemed more serious, disruptive, and/or threatening, you will need to take action to safeguard the student's safety and possibly other students' safety. In an emergency situation and when action is needed more immediately, you would call campus police (or 911) and/or your Campus Counseling Center for immediate consultation. When necessary, be sure to follow through with your observations. Ultimately, in making these decisions, use your professional experience, knowledge, sound judgment, and instincts.

The checklist chart in Figure 1.1 outlines options for faculty when responding to a student for whom they have concern.

Faculty Expectations

Faculty involvement in students' mental health is hardly a recent concern. Faculty have been recognized as valuable members of a university community who can have significant impact on student psychological well-being at least as early as the 1950s (Hardee, 1959). The change in faculty expectations over time seems to be that faculty were given more of a choice

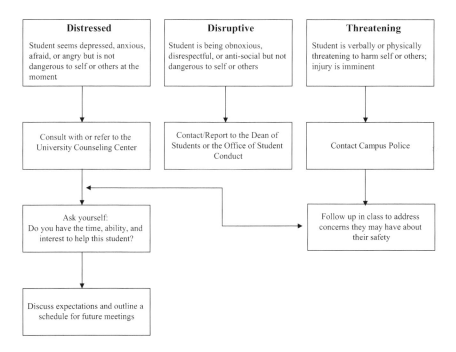

Figure 1.1 Faculty Checklist for Students of Concern

19

early on to decide if they wanted to intervene with students, while the expectation of today's college culture is for faculty and students to be engaged beyond the classroom. While faculty helping students in distress may sound like an admirable expectation, faculty are not often formally trained to take on this additional duty.

While faculty can play a critical role in the university's efforts to address college student mental health, it should be clear that faculty are not being asked to engage in activities beyond their training. Specifically, faculty are not being asked to, nor should they, make a diagnosis in order to or prior to connecting a student to mental health services. While faculty, staff, parents, and friends can be very instrumental in assisting students in locating mental health services on campus and in the community, they are not providing clinical interventions or treatment to the student. A faculty member's subjective sense that a student is distressed is sufficient to initiate a conversation with a student and to then advise the student to connect with a counseling center/mental health professional. You can encourage the student to visit a counseling center for a single session just to see if they could benefit from continued services. You can simply provide a phone number or address to the counseling center or you could allow the student to make the call for an appointment while in their office. Some faculty are comfortable walking with the student to the counseling center. All of these options are fine; it just depends on your comfort level.

Additionally, although the stigma surrounding mental health has decreased in recent years, there are still many students who do not wish to seek help for their struggles for various reasons (e.g., shame, stigma related to self and public, religious beliefs, cultural or community norms, distrust associated with sharing personal details, fear of being judged, perceived negative impact on future career, and perceived need for treatment is lower than reality). There are students who may care more about what their local reference group (peers) think than what others, in general, think (Gaddis, Ramirez, & Hernandez, 2018). Moreover, cultural considerations should also be factored into recommending and making referrals to students to seek counseling services. Cultural differences in diverse groups—ethnic, gender identity, national origin, and living circumstances—can significantly influence the perception and intensity of the stigma associated with mental health help-seeking behavior (Alegria, Atkins, Farmer, Slaton, & Stelk, 2010). For example, people in ethnic minority groups usually do not seek help when they are experiencing emotional distress but instead will use a lay referral network system (i.e., family, friends, coworkers, church group, and neighbors) rather than participating in professional mental health care (Kim, 2006). Therefore, when suggesting mental health services to students from certain cultural backgrounds, be aware that there is a possibility of reluctance and concerns about seeking and receiving professional help.

Curiosity is Great but Leave the Diagnosis to the Professionals

Many factors can influence the accuracy of a psychological diagnosis. For example, individuals will distort or suppress information during an assessment session to appear healthier, to protect family or friends, or to avoid what they fear could be more severe consequences (e.g., hospitalization, removed from residence hall, dismissed from university) (Aboraya, Rankin, France, El-Missiry, & Collin, 2006). Few individuals present in "textbook" fashion; therefore, each student will have his/her own atypical or idiosyncratic presentation of symptoms and complaints.

Faculty are not expected to diagnose a mental illness, rather, they are called to recognize when a student is in distress (Gooblar, 2018). You do not have to be a medical doctor to advise a student to seek medical attention for complaints about pain, swelling, or diminished body functions. You do not have to make a medical diagnosis before you help a student find a physician and make an appointment. Nor do you have to make a diagnosis before you call an ambulance. Likewise, you do not need to assign a diagnosis to a student before referring them to a trained mental health professional. You should focus on reporting observations and behaviors. Of course, curious faculty who want to know more about particular disorders should feel free to seek out educational programs and materials for the sake of quenching their curiosity.

Recommending and Making a Referral for Professional Counseling Services

One of the first steps in working with a distressed student is simply listening. Basic listening skills and presence will go a very long way in assessing the magnitude of the student's distress. In most cases of distress, a pair of listening ears and someone else's attunement can help decrease the intensity of the perceived stress. If after spending time listening and asking thoughtful questions the student is not able to resolve their presenting issue or calm themselves, the next step can be a referral for support services or a consultation for you—i.e., with another faculty member, the university counseling center, or the behavioral intervention team. Your consultation can help you determine what to do next and if more follow up is needed.

If during the conversation with the student you determine that a recommendation to professional counseling services is warranted, you

21

Table 1.2 Recommendations for Referring a Student to Counseling Services.

Allow the student to tell their story at their own pace and use helping skills (as discussed in Chapter 2) to facilitate the conversation. For example, asking open-ended questions encourages the student to process their thoughts and feelings and they can respond in way that is varied and expansive. Open-ended questions also allow them to reveal what they see fit, depending on their comfort level. Open-ended questions can begin with phrases such as:

- *How do you feel about …*
- *What are your thoughts about …*
- *How important is …*

For example, you could ask: "*How are other parts of your life affected*?"

Restate what you have heard (main points and common themes) and ask the student what they think would help.
　For example, you could ask, "*What do you believe that you need to do to feel better*?"

Be cognizant of how you frame the suggestion for seeking counseling services and use a tone of concern and care as you converse. Rather than saying, "*I think you need psychological help*," you can frame the referral in a way that can make the student feel less defensive or targeted. For example, you could say,

> *Based on our conversation, it sounds like you have been under a lot of stress. A lot of students have found it helpful to make an appointment with the Counseling Center. You can talk about what is going on and get some ideas on how to make things better. I would be willing to help you get an appointment. Would that be okay?*

Provide the name, phone number, and office location of the referral resource or, if you are comfortable in doing so, offer to walk with the student to the location.

Avoid making promises of confidentiality, particularly if the student presents a safety risk and especially since students who are suicidal need more direct and immediate professional intervention.

It is fine if the student indicates that they will think about seeking professional counseling services when you make a recommendation or offer referral information. Students have varying levels of distress and will sometimes deny their problems because it is difficult for them to admit they need help, believe they will get better on their own or through other sources, or have a stigma about counseling. Unless the student is suicidal or may be a danger to others, the ultimate decision belongs to the student.

End the conversation in a way that will allow you to follow up with the student.

Talk with someone in your college—academic advising office, Dean, etc., about the conversation and document your actions. Since dealing with disruptive or distressed students can be psychologically and emotionally difficult, it can be very helpful to have a discussion to debrief with a colleague, supervisor, or a professional counselor.

need to listen actively, exhibit care, and offer the resource referral information. Table 1.2 gives some recommendations to guide you through this process.

　The bottom line is that the decision to obtain counseling services resides with the student and if the student refuses the idea of counseling, it is best not to push them. Exhibiting genuineness and support when recommending professional counseling is also essential. Referrals are rarely successful when the student perceives that the person making the referral is judgmental or condescending toward them.

It is also important to understand the systemic nature of university counseling centers. You may be surprised to learn that university counseling centers do not have authority or duty related to "students." They do, however, have incredible authority and duty related to serving "clients." That is, the student is viewed as a client. Therefore, if a faculty member calls a counseling center and says, "I have a student who is talking about suicide," there is very little that the center can do other than encourage the faculty member to recommend/refer and contact the Dean of Students or the Student Conduct office. These two entities have authority and responsibility to reach out to students and make inquiries about mental health. In other words, as much as a faculty member would like to handle the situation by transferring the student to the counseling center, which is almost always a good idea, faculty are often frustrated when they call a counseling center and are told that the center cannot reach out to the student uninvited.

University counseling centers are still perceived by the campus as departments that operate "in loco parentis" and can be seen as having authority to directly intervene in students' lives. They actually do not. Furthermore, some faculty may be convinced that FERPA prevents them from talking to the counseling center, Dean of Students, or director of Student Conduct about a student. It does not.

It is also important to note that small institutions of higher education tend to have small counseling centers, often related to the budget for the most part, or they do not have a counseling center at all. Therefore, smaller institutions might offer a limited number of sessions or refer students with chronic mental health issues to external agencies, and could also choose to contract with an outside provider for students to receive mental health services via licensed professionals (which could include additional costs for the student). Therefore, it is beneficial for faculty to discover the process and where students are to obtain mental health counseling services before recommending or referring.

Addressing Suicidal Ideations and Intentions with a Student

If a student says to you that they are contemplating suicide, in spite of any discomfort, use basic helping skills to listen and suspend judgment. Remember, you are not conducting a therapy session. The goal is to engage the student in a conversation about their suicidal ideations and intentions.

You can inquire about their history with suicidal attempts, current level of distress, and plans for suicide. You simply want to encourage the student to talk about their thoughts and feelings. This will help bring more concreteness to the situation. In short, listen, suspend judgment, and gather information by asking questions like:

- Have you ever thought of harming or killing yourself before?
- What made you decide not to?
- How would you kill yourself? Do you have a plan?
- Do you have the means (e.g., pills, gun) to follow through?
- Who is someone you can contact in case you feel this way again?
- On a scale of 1 to 10, 10 being you will commit suicide and 1 being that you definitely will not, where would you rate your intent to kill yourself?

Once you have an idea of the student's intention regarding suicide, encourage them to make immediate contact with a professional mental health service provider. Offer to assist with the process, even by offering to call the counseling center to make an appointment or walking them to the office. Do not leave the student alone if you believe they are in imminent or immediate danger. Before leaving them, try to ensure that they will indeed seek professional help and/or connect with appropriate professionals to provide safety and begin treatment for being suicidal. If the student does not want to abandon the suicide plan and/or refuses to make contact with a professional counselor, as uncomfortable as this situation may be, you need to contact any available authority to step in and see to the safety of the student. Doing so means you might call local law enforcement and report that the person has a plan to commit suicide and law enforcement will intervene, possibly initiating involuntary hospitalization for the student if they believe the student is at risk for suicide.

The diagram in Figure 1.2 illustrates a process for suicide intervention that includes hospitalization. This chart is used by housing and residence life staff at our institution to decide when to have a student transported to a hospital and when to allow a student to stay on campus. It is presented here to provide some general information about the decision-making process. Faculty would not be expected to work directly with a student regarding hospitalization; they would want to contact the Dean of Students directly and let the Dean enlist the counseling center or conduct office to make contact with the student. Nonetheless, the chart below is presented merely to illustrate the variables that go into deciding if a student needs to be hospitalized.

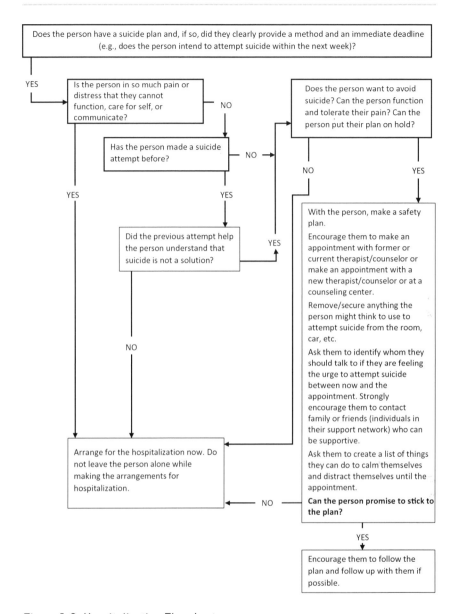

Does the person have a suicide plan and, if so, did they clearly provide a method and an immediate deadline (e.g., does the person intend to attempt suicide within the next week)?

YES

Is the person in so much pain or distress that they cannot function, care for self, or communicate?

NO

Does the person want to avoid suicide? Can the person function and tolerate their pain? Can the person put their plan on hold?

Has the person made a suicide attempt before?

NO

NO   YES

YES   YES

Did the previous attempt help the person understand that suicide is not a solution?

YES

With the person, make a safety plan.

Encourage them to make an appointment with former or current therapist/counselor or make an appointment with a new therapist/counselor or at a counseling center.

Remove/secure anything the person might think to use to attempt suicide from the room, car, etc.

Ask them to identify whom they should talk to if they are feeling the urge to attempt suicide between now and the appointment. Strongly encourage them to contact family or friends (individuals in their support network) who can be supportive.

Ask them to create a list of things they can do to calm themselves and distract themselves until the appointment.

NO

Arrange for the hospitalization now. Do not leave the person alone while making the arrangements for hospitalization.

NO

Can the person promise to stick to the plan?

YES

Encourage them to follow the plan and follow up with them if possible.

Figure 1.2 Hospitalization Flowchart

25

Having thoughts of suicide does not necessarily mean a student should be hospitalized. Many students may have a thought of suicide but have no intention of acting on the thought. When people are extremely distressed, they may question why they want to go on living but also have no desire to be dead. So, a variety of variables are involved in making a decision about hospitalization. As indicated in the chart, the student's intent and desire to be alive are taken into consideration, as well as immediate support and the overall mental stability of the student. Again, the reader is not expected to use a chart like this to guide decisions; it is provided to illustrate the complexity of deciding about hospitalization. It also orients the reader to a process that may be used by staff involved with a student.

As a matter of informed consent, be sure to tell the student that the conversation might not remain confidential. Confidentiality is a key factor but, unlike licensed/professional counselors, faculty do not have privileged communication. That is, what a student shared with you can be shared with others and is not protected by legal standards. If the student asks you to keep the conversation confidential, let them know that they are your priority and you will do what is best for their well-being and safety and that may mean sharing what they told you with someone who can help.

Many times, those in distress will share information and ask that the recipient of the information keeps it confidential; however, often this is a cry for help. Remember, you are not expected to keep this kind of information private, nor should you.

Ways Faculty Can Prepare to Support Students in Distress

Know the resources. Obtaining information and resources that will assist you in working with students in distress is prudent. There are typically numerous resources on campus to support students—financial assistance, food pantries, low-cost student health services, legal advice, classroom accommodations, and tutoring are just a few offered on most campuses today. Faculty do not necessarily need to know where all these resources exist as long as they know someone else who is familiar with the services. The value of student services collaborating with faculty and informing faculty of their services, particularly new faculty, cannot be overstated.

Additionally, the Dean of Students, the Counseling Center staff, and/or the Office of Student Conduct should be willing and pleased to come and speak with your department about their services. As counseling centers might have the most ambiguous role or service on campus, given their need for confidentiality, a lot of good things can come from having counseling center staff visit with your department or with you to discuss distressed, disruptive, and threatening students and their services. Faculty should also know that on many campuses the main responding offices (i.e., Dean of Students, Student Conduct, Campus Police, and Counseling Center) are also in close contact with each other. Contacting one office will usually lead to the other offices being notified as needed. Even in situations where student privacy must be maintained, faculty and campus services can have productive conversations about what steps to take regarding a student of concern.

In addition, some campuses offer support groups for students and there can also be support groups in the community that can be applicable to a student's need. There are also resources online that provide information about mental health and helplines that offer support. In Table 1.3 there are resources you can refer to for information or share with students.

Table 1.3 Resources for Support.

FOR YOUR INFORMATION

American Psychological Association
www.apa.org

PsychCentral
https://psychcentral.com

National Alliance on Mental Health
www.nami.org

National Institute of Health: MedlinePlus
https://medlineplus.gov/mentalhealth.html

USAGov: Mental Health and Substance Abuse
www.usa.gov/mental-health-substance-abuse

U.S. Government: youth.gov
https://youth.gov/youth-topics/youth-mental-health

Suicide Prevention Resource Center
www.sprc.org/settings/colleges-universities

American Foundation for Suicide Prevention
https://afsp.org/find-support/resources/

FOR COLLEGE STUDENTS

The Jed Foundation
www.jedfoundation.org

ULifeline, a project of The Jed Foundation
www.ulifeline.org

27

Table 1.3 (*Continued*)

HELPLINES

National Suicide Prevention Hotline
https://suicidepreventionlifeline.org
1-800-273-8255
Free and available 24 hours a day, seven days a week, for confidential support.
You can also start a confidential online chat session.

The NAMI HelpLine
Can be reached Monday through Friday, 10 am–6 pm, ET.
1-800-950-NAMI (6264) or info@nami.org
A free, nationwide peer-support service providing information, resource referrals and support to people living with a mental health condition, their family members and caregivers, mental health providers, and the public.

SAMHSA's National Helpline
www.samhsa.gov/find-help/national-helpline
1-800-662-HELP (4357)
A confidential, free, 24-hour-a-day, 365-day-a-year, information service, in English and Spanish, for individuals and family members facing mental and/or substance use disorders. This service provides referrals to local treatment facilities, support groups, and community-based organizations.

Crisis Text Line
Text HELLO to 741,741
Free and available 24 hours a day, seven days a week.

Veteran's Crisis Line
www.veteranscrisisline.net/
You can also start a confidential online chat session at veteranscrisisline.net/get-help/chat.

ULifeline
Text "START" to 741–741 or call 1-800-273-TALK (8255)

Use the syllabus as a first step. Faculty could insert language in their syllabi that encourages students to approach the faculty member when they find themselves struggling with their mental and/or physical health during the semester. Of course, inserting such statements does not suggest that faculty are replacements for mental health professionals. Rather, they are to let students know that faculty may be accommodating to unexpected changes in a student's life, or, if they are feeling distressed, the faculty member can help them with securing resources for support. If a faculty member is not comfortable with including such statements or these are seen as unacceptable by campus leaders, they can simply include details about to whom and where to go for support if they are experiencing distress.

Inserting such statements can be helpful because various students might feel embarrassed if they are struggling, and, due to pride, anxiety, shame, and other emotions, they will put off getting help until they are too far behind in their academics. Statements encouraging students to ask for help also present as evidence that there is an ethic of care on the campus.

Take advantage of opportunities to learn more. To support students, faculty can engage in training and learning opportunities to enhance their knowledge and skillset. At some institutions, the department of counseling services offers programs that faculty can attend. In addition, academic departments in the area of mental health will at times offer workshops or educational initiatives that are open to campus constituents. There are also online programs that offer educational courses and/or certification. For example, Mental Health First (www.mentalhealthfirstaid.org/take-a-course/find-a-course) is a course that teaches its participants about how to identify, understand, and respond to mental health issues. If possible, enroll in suicide prevention/intervention training. There are many suicide prevention and intervention training programs available today such as QPR (www.qpr.com) and ASIST (www.sprc.org/bpr/section-III/applied-suicide-intervention-skills-training-asist). Such programs can provide more details about how to reduce the immediate risk of suicide and provide longer-term care for those at risk.

CONCLUDING THOUGHTS

Today's college students continue to suffer at least or as much as previous generations and may be less able to function as self-assured and autonomous individuals (Burke et al., 2017). In the end, the prevalence is evident, and faculty can expect to interact and intervene with distressed students at some point. Although professional helpers can assist students with mental health issues, faculty are often on the front line when students are facing such issues. Unfortunately, faculty are not often formally informed about the signs of distressed students and disturbing/disruptive behavior and how to use helping skills to respond to both. Responding to a student's disclosure of distress while providing support can prove to be beneficial for the student and the campus community. Thus, it is critical that those who work closely with students, such as faculty, learn how to respond to students experiencing mental health issues and employ outreach strategies to ensure student well-being and success.

As discussed throughout this book, a faculty member's subjective sense, their intuition, or, simply put, their opinion that a student is struggling with psychological distress is sufficient to begin the process of helping the student get connected. Without a doubt, a great deal of self-reflection as well as relying on appropriate resources will support faculty in making good decisions when helping distressed students. Basic helping skills, which are discussed next, can be used when talking to students who are in emotional or mental distress. These considerations and techniques can help faculty serve as good helpers for students.

29

REFERENCES

Aboraya, A., Rankin, E., France, C., El-Missiry, A., & Collin, J. (2006). The reliability of psychiatric diagnosis revisited. *Psychiatry (Edgmont)*, 3(1), 41–50.

Alegria, M., Atkins, M., Farmer, E., Slaton, E., & Stelk, W. (2010). One size does not fit all: Taking diversity, culture and context seriously. *Administration and Policy in Mental Health*, 37(1–2), 48–60. doi:10.1007/s10488-010-0283-2

Alexander, K., & Alexander, K. (2017). *Higher education law*. New York, NY: Routledge. doi:10.4324/9781315616827

Amanda, G. (2015). *Mental health and student conduct issues on college campus: A reading*. Prospect, CT: Biographical Publishing Company.

American College Health Association. (2018). *American College Health Association-National college health assessment Ii: Reference group executive summary spring 2018*. Silver Spring, MD: Author. Retrieved from www.acha.org/documents/ncha/NCHA-II_Spring_2018_Reference_Group_Executive_Summary.pdf (accessed November 11, 2019).

American Psychological 2010). Practice guideline for the assessment and treatment of patients with suicidal behaviors Association. Retrieved from https://psychiatryonline.org/pb/assets/raw/sitewide/practice_guidelines/guidelines/suicide.pdf (accessed December 5, 2019).

American Psychological Association (n.d.). What is mental illness? Retrieved from www.psychiatry.org/patients-families/what-is-mental-illness

Arria, A. M., Caldeira, K. M., Vincent, K. B., Winick, E. R., Baron, R. A., & O'Grady, K. E. (2013). Discontinuous college enrollment: Associations with substance use and mental health. *Psychiatric Services*, 64(2), 165–172. doi:10.1176/appi.ps.201200106

Barry, L. C., Wakefield, D. B., Trestman, R. L., & Conwell, Y. (2016). Active and passive suicidal ideation in older prisoners. *Crisis: The Journal of Crisis Intervention and Suicide Prevention*, 37(2), 88–94. doi:10.1027/0227-5910/a000350

Benton, S., & Benton, S. (2006). *College student mental health: Effective services and strategies across campus*. Washington, DC: National Association of Student Personnel Administrators (NASPA).

Brandy, J. M., Penckofer, S., Solari-Twadell, P. A., & Velsor-Friedrich, B. (2015). Factors predictive of depression in first-year college students. *Journal of Psychosocial Nursing and Mental Health Services*, 53(2), 38–44. doi:10.3928/02793695-20150126-03

Burke, M. G., Sauerheber, J. D., Hughey, A. W., & Laves, K. (2017). *Helping skills for working with college students: Applying counseling theory to student affairs practice*. New York, NY: Routledge.

Chapnick, R. (2012, April 16). FAU student Jonatha Carr's family tells their side of the story. *University Press*. Retrieved from www.upressonline.com/2012/04/fau-student-jonatha-carrs-family-tells-their-side-of-the-story/

Degges-White, S., & Borzumato-Gainey, C. (2013). *College student mental health: A developmental approach*. New York, NY: Springer. doi:10.1891/9780826199720

Depression. (n.d.). [Definition 1]. In APA Dictionary of Psychology [online]. Retrieved from https://dictionary.apa.org/depression (accessed on December 14, 2019).

Distress. (n.d.). [Definition 1]. In APA Dictionary of Psychology [online]. Retrieved from https://dictionary.apa.org/distress (accessed on December 14, 2019).

Eagan, K., Stolzenberg, E. B., Ramirez, J. J., Aragon, M. C., Suchard, M. R., & Hurtado, S. (2014). *The American freshman: National norms fall 2014*. Los Angeles, CA: Higher Education Research Institute, UCLA.

Eisenberg, D., Golberstein, E., & Hunt, J. B. (2009). Mental health and academic success in college. *B.E. Journal of Economic Analysis and Policy*, 9(1), Article 40. doi:10.2202/1935-1682.2191

Fink, G. (2016). Stress, definitions, mechanisms, and effects outlined: Lessons from anxiety. In G. Fink (Ed.), *Stress, concepts, cognition, emotion, and behavior: Handbook of stress* (Vol. 1, pp. 3–11). San Diego, CA: Elsevier.

Fox, J., & Burstein, H. (2010). *Violence and security on campus: From preschool through college*. Westport, CT: Praeger.

Gaddis, S. M., Ramirez, D., & Hernandez, E. L. (2018). Contextualizing public stigma: Endorsed mental health treatment stigma on college and university campuses. *Social Science & Medicine*, 197(2018), 183–191. doi:10.1016/j.socscimed.2017.11.029

Galderisi, S., Heinz, A., Kastrup, M., Beezhold, J., & Sartorius, N. (2015). Toward a new definition of mental health. *World Psychiatry: Official Journal of the World Psychiatric Association (WPA)*, 14(2), 231–233. doi:10.1002/wps.20231

Gooblar, D. (2018). *How to help a student in a mental health crisis*. Retrieved from www.chronicle.com/article/How-to-Help-a-Student-in-a/245305 (accessed December 22, 2019).

Hansen, R., & Diliberti, M. (2019). *What are threat assessment teams and how prevalent are they in public schools? National Center for Education Statistics*. Retrieved from https://nces.ed.gov/blogs/nces/post/what-are-threat-assessment-teams-and-how-prevalent-are-they-in-public-schools (accessed January 5, 2020).

Hardee, M. (1959). *The faculty in college counseling*. New York, NY: McGraw-Hill Book Company.

31

Huger, M. (Ed.). (2011). *Fostering the increased integration of students with disabilities*. San Francisco, CA: Wiley. New Directions for Student Services No. 134. doi: 10.1002/ss.390

Hunt, J., & Eisenberg, D. (2010). Mental health problems and help-seeking behavior among college students. *Journal of Adolescent Health*, 46(1), 3–10. doi:10.1016/j.jadohealth.2009.08.008

Iarovici, D. (2014). *Mental health issues and the university student*. Baltimore, MD: Johns Hopkins University Press.

Jordan, J. (1996). *ADA Americans with disabilities act compliance manual for California with 1998 supplement*. Bristol, UK: Jordan Publishing.

Kadison, R., & Digeronimo, T. F. (2004). *College of the overwhelmed: The mental health crisis and what to do about it*. San Francisco, CA: Jossey-Bass.

Kazdin, A. E., (Ed.). (2000). *Encyclopedia of psychology: 8 volume set* American Psychological Association. New York, NY: Oxford University Press.

Kim, J. M. (2006). Ethnic minority counselors as cultural brokers: Using the self as an instrument to bridge the gap. In G. Walz, J. Bleuer, & R. Yep (Eds.), *Vistas: Compelling perspectives on counseling* (pp. 77–79). Alexandria, VA: American Counseling Association.

Kitzrow, M. A. (2003). The mental health needs of today's college students: Challenges and recommendations. *NASPA Journal*, *41*(1), 646–660. doi:10.2202/0027-6014.1310

Lazarus, R. S. (1974). Psychological stress and coping in adaptation and illness. *International Journal of Psychiatry in Medicine*, 5, 321–333. doi:10.2190/T43T-84P3-QDUR-7RTP

Lazarus, R. S., & Folkman, S. (1984). *Stress, appraisal, and coping*. New York, NY: Springer.

LeViness, P., Bershad, C., & Gorman, K. (2017). *The Association for University and College Counseling Center Directors annual survey*. Retrieved from https://taucccd.memberclicks.net/assets/documents/Governance/2017%20aucccd%20survey-public-apr26.pdf (accessed January 11, 2020).

McClellan, G., & Stringer, J. (2009). *The handbook of student affairs administration* (3rd ed.). San Francisco, CA: Jossey-Bass.

Melnyk, B. M., Amaya, M., Szalacha, L. A., Hoying, J., Taylor, T., & Bowersox, K. (2015). Feasibility, acceptability, and preliminary effects of COPE online cognitive-behavioral skill-building program on mental health outcomes and academic performance in freshman college students: A randomized controlled pilot study. *Journal of Child and Adolescent Psychiatric Nursing*, 28(3), 147–154. doi:10.1111/jcap.12119

Miller, T., & Sorochty, R. (2015). *Risk management in student affairs: Foundations for safety and success*. San Francisco, CA: Wiley.

Mirowsky, J., & Ross, C. E. (2002). Selecting outcomes for the sociology of mental health: Issues of measurement and dimensionality. *Journal of Health and Social Behavior, 43*, 152–170. doi:10.2307/3090194

National Association of School Psychologists. (2015). *Threat assessment for school administrators and crisis teams. National Association of School Psychologists.* Retrieved from www.nasponline.org/resources-and-publications/resources/school-safety-and-crisis/threat-assessment-at-school/threat-assessment-for-school-administrators-and-crisis-teams

Peake, L., & Mullings, B. (2016). Critical reflections on mental and emotional distress in the academy. *ACME: An International Journal for Critical Geographies, 15*(2), 253–284. Retrieved from www.acme-journal.org/index.php/acme/article/view/1123 (accessed December 29, 2019).

Ramirez, C. (2009). *FERPA clear and simple: The college professional's guide to compliance.* San Francisco, CA: Jossey-Bass.

Reetz, D. R., Bershad, C., LeViness, P., & Whitlock, M. (2016). *The Association for University and College Counseling Center Directors annual survey.* Retrieved from https://tauccd.memberclicks.net/assets/documents/aucccd%202016%20monograph%20-%20public.pdf (accessed January 4, 2020).

Reynolds, A. (2009). *Helping college students: Developing essential support skills for student affairs practice.* San Francisco, CA: Wiley.

Rutherford, P. (2010). *Meeting the needs of diverse learners.* Alexandria, VA: Just ASK Publications.

Schneiderman, N., Ironson, G., & Siegel, S. D. (2005). Stress and health: Psychological, behavioral, and biological determinants. *Annual Review of Clinical Psychology, 1*, 607–628. doi:10.1146/annurev.clinpsy.1.102803.144141

Sharkin, B. (2010). *College students in distress: A resource guide for faculty, staff, and campus community.* New York, NY: Routledge.

Sharkin, B. (2011). *Being a college counselor on today's campus: Roles, contributions, and special challenges.* New York, NY: Routledge. doi:10.4324/9780203847961

Sokolow, B., & Lewis, W. (2016). *The book on behavioral intervention teams (BIT)* (2nd ed.). Berwyn, PA: National Behavioral Intervention Team Association.

Stephens, T., Dulberg, C., & Joubert, N. (1999). Mental health of the Canadian population: A comprehensive analysis. *Chronic Diseases in Canada, 20*(3), 118–126.

Sue, D. W., Capodilupo, C. M., Torino, G. C., Bucceri, J. M., Holder, A. M. B., Nadal, K. L., & Esquilin, M. (2007). Racial microaggressions in everyday life: Implications for clinical practice. *American Psychologist, 62*(4), 271–286. doi:10.1037/0003-066X.62.4.271

33

Sue, D. W., Lin, A. I., Torino, G. C., Capodilupo, C. M., & Rivera, D. P. (2009). Racial microaggressions and difficult dialogues on race in the classroom. *Cultural Diversity and Ethnic Minority Psychology*, *15*(2), 183–190. doi:10.1037/a0014191

U.S. Department of Education (2011, February). *The Family Educational Rights and Privacy Act: Guidance for parents*. Retrieved from www2.ed.gov/policy/gen/guid/fpco/ferpa/for-parents.pdf

U.S. Department of Labor. (2019). *Americans with disabilities act*. Retrieved from www.dol.gov/general/topic/disability/ada

Vitaliano, P. P., Maiuro, R. D., Bolton, P. A., & Armsden, G. C. (1987). A psychoepidemiologic approach to the study of disaster. *Journal of Community Psychology*, *15*(2), 99–122. doi:10.1002/1520-6629(198704)15:2 99::AID-JCOP2290150202 3.0.CO;2-Q

Wheaton, B. (2007). The twain meet: Distress, disorder and the continuing conundrum of categories (comment on Horwitz). *Health*, *11*(3), 303–319. doi:10.1177/1363459307077545

Wilson, M. (2007). Crisis training. In E. L. Zdziarski, N. Dunkel, & J. M. Rollo (Eds.), *Campus crisis management: A comprehensive guide to planning, prevention, response, and recovery* (pp. 183–204). San Francisco, CA: John Wiley & Sons.

World Health Organization. (2018, March 30). *Mental health: Strengthening our response*. Retrieved from www.who.int/news-room/fact-sheets/detail/mental-health-strengthening-our-response

Yerkes, R. M., & Dodson, J. D. (1908). The relation of strength of stimulus to rapidity of habit formation. *Journal of Comparative Neurology & Psychology*, *18*, 459–482. doi:http://dx.doi.org/10.1002/cne.920180503

Zdziarski, E. L., Rollo, J. M., & Dunkel, N. W. (2007). The crisis matrix. In E. L. Zdziarski, N. Dunkel, & J. M. Rollo (Eds.), *Campus crisis management: A comprehensive guide to planning, prevention, response, and recovery* (pp. 35–51). San Francisco, CA: John Wiley & Sons.*(Continued)*

Chapter Two

Using Basic Helping Skills When Working With Students in Distress

Monica Galloway Burke, Karl Laves, Jill Duba Sauerheber, and Aaron W. Hughey

We were approaching each other in the hallway. I smiled at you and said, "How are you?" You looked down and frowned, replying softly, "I guess I am okay." I responded, "How's that weather treating you?" This is *not* an example of good listening or good helping skills. Let's rewind this scenario and try again. We were approaching each other in the hallway. While you could have been simply in thought, you looked sad. In a concerned voice, I asked, "How are you?" You looked down and frowned, replying softly, "I guess I am okay." For a couple of moments I considered how you first appeared to me. My guess was confirmed with the sound of your voice as well as what you said. I then tailored my response accordingly, "You seem sad. What is going on? Do you want to sit down and talk about it?"

The process of helping begins with demonstrating concern and value in the other person. *Helping skills*, on the other hand, complement this process.

SOCIAL INTEREST

Good helpers have social interest. As Alfred Adler (Ansbacher & Ansbacher, 1956) said, social interest is "to see with the eyes of another, to hear with the ears of another, and to feel with the heart of another" (p. 135). Having social interest means we are interested in the well-being and experiences of others. Good helpers truly have a desire to help others live to their fullest potential. They listen long and intently enough to understand others. They pause the chatter in their head that comes to conclusions and judgments about the people they are trying to help. They can sit in silence and in uncomfortable moments with others whom they are helping.

I (third editor) had just met with a friend who lost her father very suddenly. She was broken-hearted and just talking about it moved her to tears. Think about the clichés that people hear when they lose a loved one—"He led a good life." "He is in a better place now." "At least he did not suffer." When we are patient and can hold someone else's painful, uncomfortable experience, we are helping without unnecessary words. My response to her was in my nonverbal language. I did not speak. I gazed at her lovingly. I listened. I did notice my initial desire to help her make the pain go away distracted me. My eyes even welled up with tears. I was less worried about saying the right words and more concerned about just being with her. Helping is about being connected with another person more so than it is about doing or saying anything.

UNCONDITIONAL POSITIVE REGARD

Good helpers have unconditional positive regard for others. In other words, they help regardless of the individual's choices, values, religious and spiritual beliefs, political ideology, race or ethnicity, socioeconomic status (lower or higher than our own), sexual orientation, or educational level. More importantly, they always find something positive and worthy about others whom they are helping. Consider the following:

- Think of characteristics or qualities of others (or yourself) that you struggle to accept (if you are struggling to come up with something, let your guard down because we *all* have biases). For example, are there religious affiliations that you question or disagree with? How do you perceive those who have more money than you? What do you think about "White people?" What do you think about "Black people?" What thoughts do you have about immigrants? Do you have thoughts about how a woman or a man should behave?
- How might your perceptions about this quality hinder your personal freedom in helping someone who espouses this quality? Would you tend to put more effort into your helping or would you steer away from this person? For example, some of us grew up with the idea that "having religion" meant you could get through tough, challenging, and depressing times easier than those who were not religious. If we held on to this perception, we might feel compelled to advise others to "trust God," "try religion," or "pray more." Perhaps you perceive someone as being so different from you that you could not possibly help them. When I (third editor) was in the midst of my graduate degree program in counseling, I

started seeing a much older, educated, African American woman. My first response was to refer her because as I saw it then, there was nothing similar about our experiences and there was no possible way that I was going to be of help to her—she was much older than me, a different race than me, and much more educated than me. Thank goodness for a good, caring, and assertive professor. He looked me in the eye and said something like, "Get to know her. What are you waiting for?" I can assure you that this little nudge outside of my comfort zone was the push that I needed to examine my own insecurities about those who seem different from me and the myth that good helping relationships only happen among those who share the greatest similarities.

■ What are your personal (conscious and unconscious) biases? Interestingly enough, our biases are directly connected to our personal values (which are typically formed through life experiences, both positive and negative). If a person's family tree is full of overworking and highly successful people and a good work ethic is highly valued, it would not be surprising if the person has a doctorate and continues to pursue certifications. A possible unconscious bias for this person, especially if it continues to go unchecked, is that those who do not work hard are not trying enough or are lazy. Challenging such biases is crucial in a helper's ability to extend unconditional positive regard.

■ Believe it or not, sometimes helpers assist because it is easier than engaging someone else on so-called equal terms. When we are in the role of the helper, there comes an expectation from the person who we are helping that we are wiser and more experienced. Feeling wiser and more experienced than someone else is something that many of us have relished, at least for a minute or two. What is distinctive for faculty is that a system of power and influence are innately built into your role and the classroom. How will you resist the temptation to delight in the privileged experience of being a helper? How will you put your ego aside?

RELATIONSHIP BUILDING, UNDERSTANDING, AND FACILITATING

Interactions with a student are a powerful tool in a helping relationship and, therefore, building rapport and creating an environment in which the student feels secure are essential. The quality of the relationship especially needs to be of primary concern when working with a student for whom you are concerned about a sensitive issue (Parsons, 2011).

37

As previously noted, good helpers espouse many personal qualities, including those that are expressed through social interest and showing unconditional positive regard. They also depend on a process that involves using various techniques and skills. The process might be considered to include four steps—building rapport, understanding, facilitating, and reorientation (Carlson, Watts, & Maniacci, 2006).

Relationship Building

The first step of the helping process must include building a relationship with the person you are helping. Building rapport is a must! This process begins from the moment you make eye contact. For example, take an inventory of the people you have connected with today. Did you look at them and smile or did you walk past them hoping to be left alone? A relationship also begins with nonverbal and verbal gestures such as a smile, a head nod, empathetic eyes, and/or a verbal greeting. Other nonverbal behaviors that demonstrate interest and lead towards relationship building include some of the following:

- Open and relaxed body posture including leaning in, keeping arms open and not crossed, remaining grounded rather than jittery (i.e., shaking a leg, picking at a finger).
- Head nods that demonstrate interest.
- Eye contact that is not consistently shifting.
- Open, neutral, yet caring facial expression. Remember that your facial expressions also can communicate judgment.
- Maintaining an appropriate physical distance. Physical touch should be used sparingly and with caution.

Understanding

A major component of understanding is exploring what the person you are helping is struggling with and their concerns. The goal is to identify their needs, desires, expectations, and goals, paying close attention to both verbal and nonverbal cues.

- *Encourage*. You can encourage others to continue sharing by nodding your head, repeating certain poignant words they use, and using verbal encouragers. Examples include: "Uh, huh," "Yes," "Felt nervous," and "Scared."
- *Paraphrase*. Reword parts of what someone says. For example, if they begin to cry or seem to get nervous when talking about

a particular situation, paraphrase what they were saying in that moment. Examples include: "You were crying when you said you were scared." "You said that you are very worried about your friend." "You want to go away and hide."

- *Reflection of feeling.* You can identify how others are feeling by their body posture and sometimes they will tell you how they feel. Furthermore, it is important to distinguish between feelings and thoughts. For example, if someone says, "I feel like they don't like me," they are describing a thought, not a feeling. You can take a guess about what the feeling is behind this thought based on their nonverbal cues and tone—e.g., sad, confused, awkward or disappointed. Some examples of reflections of feeling include: "You feel anxious about going back home for the holidays." "You are worried about the upcoming chemistry exam." "You are so angry and sometimes you just want to get it all out."

- *Summarize.* We use summaries to help us understand if we are hearing the essential points of what others are saying. Summaries are usually two to three sentences long and include reflection of feelings.

- *Ask open-ended questions and prompts.* Open-ended questions and prompts begin with How, What, or Tell Me More. Closed-ended questions begin with Is, Why and Who? Open-ended questions and prompts tend to elicit more in-depth responses. Closed-ended questions tend to elicit short answers such as no, yes, or I don't know. You should be intentional about the types of questions you ask. For example, if you want to essentially know if a student is attending class, you should use a closed-ended question such as "Did you attend classes this week?" However, if you wish, follow up with an open-ended question to gather relevant information and thoughts, so you could ask "What are some possible outcomes of not attending classes?" Some open-ended questions and prompts include:
  - Tell me more about feeling so angry at your roommate.
  - Tell me what the scariest part of having to go home is.
  - How did you get through the argument with your friend?
  - What happened before you blacked out?

- *Continue to use nonverbal behavior.* The following excerpt illustrates how these skills may be used.

  Helper: How are you? (*Open-ended question.*)

  Helpee: Well, I am not so good.

  Helper: Not so good. (*Encouragement by repeating of key words.*)

Helpee:	My mind is racing and I am worried that my friends think I'm a freak. We can all be laughing, but when I leave the room, they all seem to speak in a much lower tone. I immediately wonder what they are saying and if I am the topic of their conversation.
Helper:	You wonder if your friends are talking about you. (*Paraphrase.*)
Helpee:	Right. Like I'm an idiot or something. I feel like such an idiot.
Helper:	You think (*note this is a thought rather than a feeling*) that you are an idiot (*paraphrase*) and you are feeling anxious and sad about this (*reflection of feeling*).
Helpee:	Yea. I want to not care, but this is all I think about. My girlfriend tells me not to worry about it, but I can't stop these thoughts. Then I have this biology test coming up soon and a presentation next week. I guess those things are irrelevant, but everything seems to build on one other.
Helper:	Let me see if I have this right. You are really nervous and can't stop wondering if your friends are talking about you. Even though your girlfriend told you that this is not true, it's still hard to believe. (*Summary with reflection of feeling.*)

Effective questioning, paraphrasing, and reflection allow you to gain information, increase understanding, and explore the issues and concerns of the student, and this can guide the conversation which may assist the student in sharing more of the story. Using these helping skills effectively can be used to solicit information and move the student toward reflection and goal setting. Being a skilled helper also allows you to move beyond any assumptions held and help you to get clarification, which could validate your intuition.

Facilitating

Remember that the most important part of helping is communicating that you are listening. Sometimes the process of helping does not go further than simply listening and being present. You can check in with the student you are helping by saying "Sometimes it's helpful just to get things out. Was this helpful?" Furthermore, be cautious about offering advice to the student you are helping (remember that advice giving is based on your own personal values and judgment of what you think is best).

Sometimes you will need to help the student make a decision or to do something different. This process of facilitating involves helping an individual come to a different perspective as well as deciding on what steps they want to take next. While the remainder of this book will include specific directions on helping others move through an issue or crisis, some general hints include:

- Ask the student what they want to be doing differently. Refrain from assuming you know what is best for them, which can be difficult at times. Instead, ask a question such as, "In three months, what do you hope would be different in your life?" or, in a more acute situation, "What would you like to be different tomorrow?"
- Provide direction that can be supported in professional literature (e.g., this book) and/or by experts in the field. Refrain from giving advice that is solely based on your experiences and judgment. You might say something like:
  - Have you considered making an appointment with a counselor on campus?
  - When our pulse rates reach over 100 beats per minute, we are no longer thinking clearly. I wonder if we could practice some relaxation techniques.
  - When you are feeling really anxious, be sure to take lots of deep breaths.
- Help the student identify support systems (i.e., family member, friend, professor, coach). You might also help them secure a professional counseling appointment or join a support group.
  - Who are some individuals that you can trust? How can you connect with them?
- Point out exceptions. Often when we are in crisis or distress all we can see and feel is the distress. Help the person see exceptions to the situation. For example:
  - You have gotten through so many exams and have done well.
  - You mentioned that you have many good friends but are concerned only with this one.
  - Have you been able to control your anger in other situations?
  - You feel like you are going to have a panic attack, but you mentioned that you have gotten yourself out of them before.

Reorientation

Your time with those you help is temporary. Chances are that it will not be appropriate to go home with them or spend long periods of time with them. Your role is to essentially help them *reorient* themselves back into the swing of things. After you have built trust, listened to what they are struggling with, and perhaps attempted to provide direction, it is time to help the student apply what you talked about. Consider the following excerpt:

Helper: I am wondering if there is anything that you can take from what we talked about today.

Helpee: Well, I do need to start taking deep breaths. It's just that sometimes I forget in the heat of the moment.

Helper: Gosh, we all forget sometimes. What do you think could help you remember to breathe when things get really touchy?

Helpee: Well, I definitely notice that my thoughts start racing and I feel like I am going to throw up. So paying attention to that might be a good idea.

Helper: So, when all those thoughts start racing and you feel like you might throw up, you will take deep breaths. I wonder if there are other ways to remember. For example, I actually put "take deep breaths" in my calendar.

Helpee: Yes, I can do that.

Using the aforementioned techniques should be coupled with cultural considerations. As a helper, respect for the diversity of cultures and values of individuals must serve as a precondition for successful helping. Competent regard of diversity is a basic tenet underlying good helping.

CULTURAL CONSIDERATIONS FOR USING HELPING SKILLS WITH STUDENTS IN DISTRESS

Today's college campuses are filled with diverse students and culture pervades all exchanges that occur on the college campus. Kuh and Whitt (1997) defined culture as,

> The collective, mutually shaping patterns of norms, values, practices, beliefs, and assumptions that guide the behaviors of individuals and groups in an institute of higher education and provide a frame of reference within which to interpret the meaning of events and actions on and off campus.

(p. 127)

Cultures exist on various levels and cultural issues can affect the campus community, students, and relationships. Culture shapes how we perceive

42

our world and function within it; it influences our personal and group values, attitudes, and perceptions; and it helps us to understand how people interpret their environment (Geertz, 1973; Jandt, 2013; Markus, Mullally, & Kitayama, 1997; McAuliffe & Associates, 2013). As such, professionals in higher education should be aware of the power associated with dominant and subordinate cultural groups and the internal and external dimensions associated with cultural identities (e.g., gender, race, religion, socioeconomic status, and ability). Consideration should be applied to such dynamics so as to not perpetuate any marginalization or discrimination. For example, in terms of social interactions, Asians/Asian Americans are more aware of and concerned about relationship maintenance (Hashimoto, Mojaverian, & Kim, 2012) and "saving face" in public so as to avoid stigma and shame (Sue & Morishima, 1982), particularly when seeking help for personal issues is involved (Shon & Ja, 1982). Therefore, when working with an Asian or Asian American student who you believe is experiencing mental health issues, there could be more indirect communication in the conversation and a lack of interest in utilizing any type of counseling services for mental health or emotional problems due to a perception that an explicit admission of the existence of these problems may result in public shame (loss of face) to the family. This outcome could be because hierarchical relationships and obedience to authority are typically highly valued in Asian/Asian American culture, suggesting that social interaction may differ cross-culturally. Although there are within-group differences in cultural groups, there are general cultural beliefs and values that transcend specific groups. However, any generalization has to be done with caution because, although we are influenced by culture, each of us is a unique individual shaped by our experiences.

The cultural identities we all live with and live out from day to day (i.e., race, sex, gender, ability, class, and religion) in our society confirm our identities, as well as further mold our experiences and perceptions, which is why we have to be especially cognizant of how our views can impact our ability to see others' views. Furthermore, humans categorize and organize people, often creating in-groups and out-groups and, unfortunately, this otherness and categorization can be accompanied by stereotypes, prejudice, and discrimination. This actuality is why those of us who help others must be culturally self-aware. First, we should reflect upon and analyze our personal beliefs, biases, fears, worldview and attitudes, including the source of our beliefs and how they influence our perspectives. Since we use our own cultural group as a reference and standard of normality (Hays & Erford, 2014), we must be careful to avoid having a narrow and rigid view of the world and cultural backgrounds that differ from ours. You should evaluate your biases and stereotypes, acknowledge cultural perspectives,

43

and recognize ways in which your personal biases and values can affect how you develop rapport with and help students who are culturally different. This evaluation requires an honest reflection on your part, acknowledging how your cultural background influences your thoughts and behaviors. Of course, being honest with yourself and engaging in reflection can be an uncomfortable and extended process.

You should also try to consider *what it means for the student* to identify with a specific cultural group. For example, students who identify with underrepresented and/or marginalized groups may have likely encountered experiences associated with power, privilege, and discrimination which consequently have shaped their perspectives. Consider religious or spiritual identifications. On the one hand, research suggests that religion and spirituality are positively correlated with coping with stress (Graham, Furr, Flowers, & Burke, 2001; Park, 2013), however this is not always the case. Many of us have been hurt by or have experienced emotional pressure from religious groups. For example, if someone is wearing a cross, do not assume that their experience and/or perceptions about Christianity are the same as yours. We can also say something similar about one's familial relationships. Sometimes a student's family is the cause of the distress. In other situations students have supportive families, but the student is ashamed to ask for help. Do not assume you understand the context of a student's relationships with his or her family members.

The complex intersection of our identities (e.g., Latino, gay, male, able-bodied, Catholic student with an anxiety disorder) accompanies each of us in every social interaction and the saliency of these identities becomes more apparent and poignant in situations where we are in a minority or subordinate status. Therefore, on a predominantly White college campus, this manifestation is especially palpable as the campus culture can present challenges for minority students such as feeling marginalized and excluded from campus social networks to which their White peers have access and dealing with pressures to represent their race and assimilate to the majority culture of their campus (Lewis, Chesler, & Forman, 2000). For example, if a White professor is discussing characteristics of high-poverty neighborhoods and ghettos during class and turns to ask a Black student if they would not mind sharing their experiences about living in such environments while not knowing any of the student's background, they are basing their comment on preconceived notions. This type of behavior, such as asking a student to serve as the "native informant," can be physically, emotionally, and psychologically exhausting for the student and erode the trust the student has for the faculty as well as their sense of belonging in the classroom. This interaction also negatively affects their sense of belonging, perception of cross-racial interactions, and degree completion (Hurtado,

Alvarez, Guillermo-Wann, Cuellar, & Arellano, 2012). It may not have been the professor's intention to embarrass or offend the student, but the impact can nonetheless be devastating and disconcerting for the student. Additionally, such thoughts and behaviors exhibited by faculty can impede their ability to be accepting and work effectively with certain students.

What can also add to the distress is for the student's feelings to be dismissed or to be accused of being hypersensitive if they inform the faculty they are upset by the exchange in class and with the faculty member. For example, a reply such as "Don't be too sensitive about the race stuff. I didn't mean anything bad by it" aligns itself with a blame-the-victim stance. A colorblind ideology, such as replying "I don't see you as Black. I just see you as a normal student like every other" can also communicate indifference, a view of abnormality in being Black in our society, and ignore the reality of the student's experience and living their life with an identity in a subordinate status. If faculty are to foster a welcoming environment for all students, they must be aware, able to sit with discomfort, and attempt to personally avoid as well as anticipate defensive reactions when difficult dialogues related to diversity arise—e.g., arguing against the existence of the injustice; deflecting the focus toward a less threatening topic; providing a logical response or alternative reason why societal injustices occur; focusing on personal acts of goodwill rather than the issue at hand; or shifting the issue down to simple facts (Watt, 2007). Experiencing such psychological stressors and microaggressions often, whether it is overt or covert, has an effect on a student's well-being and energy.

In summary, concepts and experiences related to cultural diversity require that faculty who help culturally diverse students in emotional distress have an awareness, including self-awareness, related to cultural backgrounds, biases, cultural beliefs, and stigma. Further, doing so will also require that faculty remain open-minded, reflective, and flexible to better assist the student who needs help.

KNOWING WHEN AND WHAT TO DO

Helping skills are great to use when a student is engaging in behavior that causes concern. If you can remember to remain as calm as possible and effectively incorporate the aforementioned helping skills when conversing with the student in distress, the helping process can seem more like a natural process. However, you must remember that there are times when what is required is beyond you using helping skills to help a student in distress. You must observe and determine if the student's behavior is potentially harmful to you or others. A student may demonstrate concerning behavior, but it may not necessarily be alarming or threatening in nature or a

45

violation of policy. Concerning behavior (e.g., a student gives unwanted attention that violates personal space; a student exhibits poor social skills or is unable to read social cues; a student makes inappropriate statements) may simply result in you having a conversation with the student and possibly providing a warning. If a student's behavior is eliciting concern or if you are worried that the student is distressed, depressed, anxious, or suicidal, but the behavior is not disrupting class or threatening to faculty or other students, contacting the counseling center for a consultation is advised. The counseling center can do two things in this situation—they can give the faculty member advice on how to interact with the student including offering help with a referral, or they can take information about the student and share it with the campus committee responsible for monitoring students of concern. Sharing information allows other offices like student conduct or dean of students to be aware of students in need. These other offices might also be able to provide assistance to the faculty member or student in need.

Faculty should remember, as mentioned previously, that FERPA does not prevent timely communication between university personnel on matters of student behavior. It is acceptable for a faculty member to talk to someone at the counseling center about a student. Ultimately, the student's well-being takes priority and any concern about privacy and FERPA applies to student records (e.g., grades, test scores, disciplinary records). FERPA does not apply to whatever a faculty member has heard or observed from a student. Counseling centers are more limited in what they can share with a faculty member, but counseling centers can take in any and all information that a faculty member wants to share. Counseling centers are limited in what they can say to faculty about a particular student because they are required by law in most states to have student permission before speaking specifically about a student. For example, if faculty member Jones calls counseling psychologist Laves to talk about student Smith and Laves happens to know that Smith is a client at the center, Laves cannot tell Jones that Smith is a client or that Smith is being seen by a counselor. Laves would need Smith's permission to share that information with Jones, but Laves can listen to Jones. Counseling centers are ethically and legally obligated to act on information that is shared by faculty, but counseling centers cannot share anything with the faculty member that might identify the student as a client.

There is a cause for more action if a student is exhibiting alarming behavior (e.g., a student sends offensive or inappropriate e-mails, text messages, or social media messages to others; a student persistently violates personal space; or a student displays unwarranted or repeated anger or outbursts or damaging behavior), or threatening behavior (e.g., a student is verbally aggressive and seems irrational; a student implies or makes a direct threat to harm themselves or others; a student physically confronts/attacks another individual; a student stalks or harasses another individual on campus). If a student's behavior is disruptive, in violation of the student code of conduct, or is rude, insensitive, or upsetting to others, the faculty should contact the Dean of Students or the Office of Student Conduct. Faculty need to be aware of the student code of conduct to know what is considered inappropriate behavior in the classroom and on campus. On many campuses, the Dean of Students and the Counseling Center work closely together. The Dean of Students might decide that a disruptive student is also in need of counseling. In that case, the Dean of Students will make a referral to the Counseling Center; but even if the student could benefit from counseling, they still need to be held accountable to the institution's code of conduct. Rarely is a psychological issue or disorder grounds for tolerating disruptive behavior.

If a student's behavior is threatening, the faculty member should immediately contact campus police or local law enforcement. If a student is making verbal threats to harm themselves or others or if the student is engaging in behavior that could harm themselves or others, then all concerns about the student's need for counseling or discipline take a back seat to the immediate reality of someone being injured or killed. Campus police are the best trained professionals for situations that involve threat or harm. Campus police can always consult with the Dean of Students (or the counseling center) once they have arrived on scene and have seen to the security of the threatening student and the classroom/campus. It is always a good idea to have the campus police number saved in your cell phone if you have one (and to keep it near you in the classroom). If you see a pattern in behavior that is alarming and leaning toward threatening or is threatening, document and keep thorough records (which includes exact words, actions, date, time, behavior, witnesses, and personal reactions if pertinent). Having documentation could be handy if the issues escalate. In the end, the goal is to not only help the student but to also ensure the safety and well-being of you and others around you.

Similarly, faculty need to be comfortable with the idea that, if necessary, they will need to contact campus police to intervene and detain or arrest a student who is threatening. Whether the student is actually dangerous can be determined later once officers have arrived. Given the incidents of violence on college campuses today, a faculty member is justified in calling the police. As the old saying goes, "better safe than sorry." Even a student with a known disorder is not justified in acting out in an aggressive and threatening manner. Threats do not need to be tolerated and threats should never be tolerated. Additionally, if you believe the student might harm

47

themselves or others, then the best thing to do is to call campus police or local law enforcement. It might be helpful to inform students that, if necessary, you will ensure student safety by calling campus police to your office or classroom.

Faculty may also find that they need advice or support as they continue working with a particular student. As the semester progresses, a student may develop new concerns and the faculty member might feel lost or unsure of their next steps. Establishing a working relationship directly with a counseling center can come in handy later. Note that counseling centers will vary in their availability and interest in providing consultation or advice for faculty. It would be worth a faculty member's time to see if the campus counseling center would provide additional consultation over time.

CONCLUDING THOUGHTS

College students often experience high levels of stress, sadness, conflict, and personal challenges that can derail them psychologically and profoundly affect their emotional health, physical health, behavior, and academic performance. Some students lose their ability to cope, contemplate dropping out of college, or have thoughts of harming themselves or others. Faculty are tasked with teaching, advising, and enhancing the academic life of students, but, if a student is not functioning well psychologically and emotionally, their academic success is in jeopardy. When a student is in distress, figuring out a way to help them can leave faculty troubled and wondering what approach would work best.

To help students during challenging times, faculty should be provided with the approaches, tools, techniques, and strategies needed to recognize alarming behavior, provide quality support, and enhance students' overall well-being. Using helping skills effectively is one way for faculty to interact with students in distress and gather enough information to identify when a student is in crisis. However, when helping a student in need, no matter how gratifying the experience can be, faculty must recognize to what lengths they should go, making sure to remain within realistic limits. Faculty must express their limitations and maintain boundaries as they are not expected to be a professional counselor but serve an important role as a link to resources for the student. There are trained professionals who are available to help; therefore, when dealing with students in distress, faculty must also be sure to know when to consult, refer, and ensure the safety of the student and others.

REFERENCES

Ansbacher, H. L., & Ansbacher, R. R. (Eds.). (1956). *The individual psychology of Alfred Adler: A systemic presentation in selections from his writings*. New York, NY: Basic Books.

Carlson, J., Watts, R., & Maniacci, M. (2006). *Adlerian therapy*. Washington, DC: American Psychological Association.

Eisenberg, D., Golberstein, E., & Hunt, J. B. (2009). Mental health and academic success in college. *B.E. Journal of Economic Analysis and Policy*, 9(1), Article 40, doi: 10.2202/1935-1682.2191.

Geertz, C. (1973). *The interpretation of cultures*. New York, NY: Basic Books.

Graham, S., Furr, S., Flowers, C., & Burke, M. T. (2001). Religion and spirituality in coping with stress. *Counseling and Values*, 46(1), 2–13. doi:10.1002/j.2161-007X.2001.tb00202.x

Hashimoto, T., Mojaverian, T., & Kim, H. S. (2012). Culture, interpersonal stress, and psychological distress. *Journal of Cross-Cultural Psychology*, 43(4), 527–532. doi:10.1177/0022022112438396

Hays, D. G., & Erford, B. T. (2014). *Developing multicultural counseling competence: A systems approach* (2nd ed.). Boston, MA: Pearson.

Hurtado, S., Alvarez, C. L., Guillermo-Wann, C., Cuellar, M., & Arellano, L. (2012). A model for diverse learning environments: The scholarship on creating and assessing conditions for student success. In J. C. Smart, & M. B. Paulsen (Eds.), *Higher education: Handbook of theory and research* (Vol. 27, pp. 41–122.). Dordrecht, Netherlands: Springer.

Jandt, F. E. (2013). *An introduction to intercultural communication: Identities in a global community* (7th ed.). Los Angeles, CA: Sage Publications.

Kuh, G. D., & Whitt, E. J. (1997). The invisible tapestry: Culture in American colleges and universities. Culture defined and described. In E. J. Whitt (Ed.), *College student affairs administration* (pp. 125–135). Needham Heights, MA: Simon & Schuster Custom Publishing.

Lewis, A. E., Chesler, M., & Forman, T. A. (2000). The impact of "colorblind" ideologies on students of color: Intergroup relations at a predominantly White university. *Journal of Negro Education*, 69(1–2), 74–91.

Markus, H. R., Mullally, P. R., & Kitayama, S. (1997). Selfways: Diversity in modes of cultural participation. In U. Neisser, & D. Jopling (Eds.), *The conceptual self in context: Culture, experience, self-understanding* (pp. 13–61). New York, NY: Cambridge University Press.

McAuliffe, G. & Associates. (2013). *Culturally alert counseling: A comprehensive introduction* (2nd ed.). Los Angeles, CA: Sage.

Park, C. L. (2013). Religion and meaning. In R. F. Paloutzian, & C. L. Park (Eds.), *Handbook of the psychology of religion and spirituality* (pp. 357–378). New York, NY: The Guilford Press.

Parsons, R. D. (2011). *Fundamentals of the helping process* (2nd ed.). Long Grove, IL: Waveland Press, Inc.

Shon, S. P., & Ja, D. Y. (1982). Asian families. In M. McGoldrick, J. K. Pearce, & J. Giordano (Eds.), *Ethnicity and family therapy* (pp. 208–228). New York, NY: Guilford.

Sue, S., & Morishima, J. K. (1982). *The mental health of Asian Americans* (1st ed.). San Francisco, CA: Jossey-Bass.

Watt, S. K. (2007). Difficult dialogues, privilege and social justice: Uses of the privileged identity exploration (PIE) model in student affairs practice. *College Student Affairs Journal, 26*(2), 114–126.

Part II

Sharing Their Stories

Faculty Helping Students in Distress

Chapter Three

Coping Amidst Life Events and Mental Distress

Colin Cannonier

INTRODUCTION

According to the World Health Organization (WHO, 2019), mental health is one of the leading causes of illness among adolescents, half of whom are affected by the time they reach the age of 14. Significantly, the majority of the adolescents with mental health issues go undiagnosed or untreated. Depression among adolescents is one of the associated illnesses which can ultimately cause death, oftentimes by suicide. Like the rest of the world, mental illness is one of the more common forms of illnesses in the United States. Amongst individuals between the ages 15 to 29, depression and other mental and behavioral disorders in the US account for approximately 660 fewer years (per 100,000 people) of healthy life (WHO, 2018).[1] Data from the National Institute of Mental Health (NIMH, 2019) indicate there are about 50 million Americans who are living with a mental health illness to some varying degree, representing about 20 percent of the nation's population. Mental health conditions extend well into adulthood and are most prevalent among those in the 18 to 25 age group, who also receive the least amount of treatment (NIMH, 2019). The problems associated with mental health illness are unrelenting.

HIGHER EDUCATION AND MENTAL HEALTH

With over 40 percent of adults 18 to 25 enrolling in colleges in the US (U.S. Department of Education, 2018), higher education can play a pivotal role in lessening the effects of mental health. For one thing, there is a wide and expanding literature linking the onset of mental illness and early adulthood, in particular among undergraduate students (Hussain, Guppy, Robertson, & Temple, 2013). Also, in many cases, the college environment provides certain conditions (e.g., stigma, peer pressure, bullying and other stressful situations) over a sufficiently long period of time that may exacerbate or increase the risk of developing mental illness among this vulnerable group (Mirowsky & Ross, 2003).

An expanding literature documents that those with higher education have fewer symptoms of depression (Quesnel-Vallée & Taylor, 2012). Higher levels of education can aid mental health by equipping those distressed with the information required to successfully combat stressors (Mirowsky & Ross, 2003). The argument goes as follows: To the extent that those with higher education are conferred with economic, occupational, and status awards, these achievements can improve self-esteem, lessen financial difficulties, and afford individuals the resources necessary to minimize and avoid some of the psychological stressors that may otherwise be evident in the absence of some of these benefits. Although higher education is widely recognized and accepted as playing a crucial role in human capital development, its link to mental health in particular is less well understood. A host of factors have been known to influence both higher education and mental health. These include family circumstances, socioeconomic status, neighborhood effects, genetics, environment and individual characteristics such as sex, gender identity, race, and ethnicity and so on. Further, the timing and duration of these factors across the life cycle are important to better understand the mechanisms through which higher education and mental health impact each other. A critical challenge faced by higher education faculty and staff is how to deal with mental health issues among students who they are already helping in their pursuit of higher education. The next section provides some context to the nature and type of environment in which faculty in higher education operates when having to play a dual role of teacher and helper.

BACKGROUND INFORMATION

In 2010 a young, White, and vibrant individual began a journey in higher education right after graduating from high school. This individual is hereafter referred to as "CMZ."[2] CMZ lived with his mother and stepfather, who succumbed to a heart attack about a month prior to his graduation from high school. At an early age, CMZ felt he was born to serve the community and as he began his college career, he pursued a degree with a major that was in alignment with this perceived calling. He was feeling fulfilled and was enjoying the opportunity to learn and acquire knowledge at his first institution of higher education. However, another challenge soon confronted CMZ— his mother was diagnosed with a terminal illness that had progressed to an advanced stage. For the next several years, CMZ took care of his mom and continued to attend school. Eventually, this routine became unsustainable and CMZ decided to put more focus into caring for his sick mother and made the decision to become a college dropout, albeit temporarily. To be clear, I had no knowledge of this information prior to our interactions which I describe below.

SETTING/CONTEXT

My first encounter with CMZ occurred when he decided to re-enter higher education in another major. CMZ, now a sophomore, was once again a full-time student taking classes at the undergraduate level and was pursuing a major which required taking one of my principal-level courses. The class met on Tuesdays and Thursdays and was taught via the traditional method during the day. CMZ was always on time and usually sat in one of the front-row seats located by the lecture podium. He was keen on seeking solutions to questions that were of relevance to society and people in general. One Friday afternoon, nearing the end of the semester, I received an email from CMZ who wanted to provide an explanation for why he was absent from the previous classes. According to CMZ, he spent both days with his mother at several appointments as she was dealing with a severe illness which, by all accounts, had a dire prognosis. CMZ promised to return to class the following Tuesday. I responded immediately to CMZ's email, thanking him for providing an update and sincerely hoping that he and his family were able to work through this particular challenge and wishing that his mom receives a better than expected prognosis. CMZ was also encouraged to reach out to me with any questions.

Over the remaining six class meetings, CMZ was absent for all but one and did not show up for the final exam at the end of the semester. At the time, I felt the student was dealing with a sufficiently serious issue to be given *excused* absences which would not count against his class performance.[3] By doing so, I left open the opportunity for the student to complete the class by taking the final exam in a subsequent semester. My final grade submission of an "incomplete" was in keeping with such a possibility. At no point did it occur to me to consult with others about the student's issue. It was my assumption that the student would be in contact with the relevant university officials regarding his family situation.

The following semester, I was somewhat surprised to see CMZ on one of my class rosters. CMZ was repeating the class! I spoke briefly to CMZ on the first day of class and privately asked if things were going well. Nevertheless, the semester proceeded and it appeared that CMZ was making positive strides similar to the previous semester. As the semester approached the half-way mark, I noticed that CMZ had been absent for the previous three class meetings and another following the Fall Break. I proceeded to contact him by email to get a sense of his well-being. Specifically, I wrote

55

and asked him how he was doing and also let him know the reason I was reaching out was because we missed him during the recent class meetings. The email concluded by letting him know I was hoping that he was doing okay and offered the opportunity for him to reach out to me if I could be of any assistance. I believe my previous interactions with CMZ alerted me to reach out as soon as I thought it was necessary to do so.

CMZ sent a reply email three days later, thanking me for reaching out and apologizing for not contacting me sooner. In a candid response, CMZ indicated his recent struggles with mental health as he was diagnosed with a form of bipolar disorder and was in the process of deciding to get the requisite medication to get him back to a normal state of mind. CMZ admitted that it was a challenge to be in a frame of mind that would allow him to get his assignments done. The situation had progressed to a stage where his doctor's recommendation was to sit out the remainder of the semester and focus on getting well again. CMZ noted that he was disappointed with himself and wanted to prove to me "how great of a student [he] can be when ... not distracted by life events or health ... It speaks volumes of you that you are concerned about students and reach out to them to offer assistance." I responded to CMZ, letting him know that I was glad to hear from him and equally delighted that he was seeking the necessary medical attention. I assured him that I was well aware of his potential and was never in need of further proof. Further, I assured him that I was available to assist wherever possible and asked him to remain in touch. CMZ eventually withdrew from the course. I believe this was my first experience in dealing with a student who I knew was dealing with mental health issues.

This experience had left an indelible impression on me because, three years later, I reached out to CMZ, who was no longer a student at the institution, to touch base. Below is an excerpt of the conversation:

Author: Hello CMZ! This is one of your professors at [name of institution – Author's full name]. We last connected in [year] regarding your mom. It has been a while but I wanted to know how you were doing. Looking forward to hearing from you.

CMZ: Oh wow great memory on your part! I am doing well, my father unexpectedly passed away in [month] from [name of illness]. Other than that I have been living my best life and loving work. I'm the ... manager at a ... Thanks for checking in! I trust things are well for you?

Author: Great to hear from you! ... I am certainly happy that you are living your best life, but sorry to hear about the recent passing of your father. By the way, how is your mother?

CMZ: My mother has since lost her battle ....

RECOMMENDATIONS AND CONCLUSION

There are several recommendations that I offer based on the situation illustrated above. First, it will benefit faculty to be informed of the initial steps that can be taken to provide a pathway of help for students suffering with mental health issues. For example, something as basic as communicating with students about contacting the Dean of Students or providing the contact information for relevant student health services may seem a trivial affair. Truth be told, many faculty are already absorbed in other areas of their work so that, oftentimes, making this information available at the outset to students is not one of the first things that comes to mind. It took me several years and numerous conversations with faculty with expertise in the area of mental health to be able to provide more effective information to students as a normal course of duty. For example, these days, as soon as I have sufficient information from a student to suggest they might be in danger of suffering from a mental health issue that may be adversely affecting class performance and general well-being, I have now learned to reach out to the student with the type of information as shown below:

Dear [Student]:

I am sorry to hear about the difficulties you are experiencing in your life. If you have not already done so, I suggest you contact the Dean of Student's Office (telephone [insert telephone number here]; website: [insert relevant link to the website here]) which can assist you with this matter for all of your courses.

Since emotional/mental well-being is important to our daily functioning, I kindly recommend you seek support and assistance from a qualified health professional who is trained in these matters. The university provides free and confidential services to students. Walk-In Hours are Monday through Friday 10:00 am to 3:00 pm. Their contact information is [insert telephone number here] or email [insert email address here]. They are located in the [insert physical location here]. Here is a link to their page: [insert website link here].

In addition, I also reach out to the Dean of Students or the equivalent to alert and inform them that a student might be suffering from a mental health issue.

57

Second, providing pertinent information—such as contact information for student health clinics on whiteboards or bulletin boards in classrooms—can be effective in spreading important health information to students who are inclined to follow through with constant reminders of where to go when in need of help. Students are more apt to remember information when it is provided on the spot and are less likely to revert to their syllabus or some other inventory of information that they would have received during orientation. Third, it behooves faculty to constantly consult with other faculty as well as administrators on the various avenues that can be pursued when a student reaches out for help.

Based on my experiences with CMZ as well as other students in distress, there are some factors that, if monitored carefully, can provide sufficient information as to warning signs that a student may be in distress. One such indicator is attendance. While policies on attendance vary across higher education institutions, taking attendance at every class can help a faculty detect trends in student's participation in class. In the case of CMZ, I reached out to the student after observing three consecutive absences. Another indicator is a student's performance on assignments. CMZ's performance in class assignments had decreased progressively to the point where there was a 5-letter grade difference between the first and second test scores.

The above narrative provides additional support for those who argue for greater information sharing or even training of faculty in higher education to help combat the adverse effects of mental health illness on campus. Whether and under what conditions can this potential increase in faculty responsibility be undertaken should be a key question deserving greater attention. At the same time, to better achieve policy goals, it is imperative that we know more about the underlying mechanisms that are responsible for the spate of mental health illness evident in higher education institutions.

TAKEAWAYS

- Some students will experience compounding factors that contribute to their distress, as in this narrative, which could further impede their ability to cope and their academic success. It is important that faculty view their interactions with distressed students as constantly evolving and be open to the very real idea that there is often more going on in a student's life than is evident in the immediate situation.
- Consulting with faculty who have more experience and knowledge about support resources for students in distress can be an effective

way to increase your knowledge base. We can all learn from those who have first-hand experience dealing with distressed students. Keep in mind, however, that every encounter is going to be unique and what works in one situation might not work as well (or at all) in a different situation.

■ If responding to a student in distress via email, including information such as the policies related to excused excessive absences and academic withdrawal as well as support services on campus can be beneficial. At the same time, this information should not distract from the primary goal of helping the student through their immediate circumstances.

■ Using email to conduct a periodic "check in" after meeting with students, which is certainly an increase in your time and tasks, can create appreciation among students and might make it easier for students to seek information or referrals from you. However, always be mindful of the limitations of electronic communication, which can never replace face-to-face communication.

■ Excessive and/or consistent absences can warrant a follow-up question to a student about their well-being. A simple statement to a student, while out of the listening range of others, might be, "You have missed a few classes, I hope all is well. Is there something going on that is keeping you from attending class consistently?" Such communication can also be done via email. It is also important to note that not every student wants to be helped or believes there is an issue.

■ Being engaging and encouraging are great responses to students in distress; but offering resources to them for assistance is more important. You do not want students just to feel good, you want them to actually be good. It could be advantageous to have a list of resources on campus available just in case.

QUESTIONS FOR REFLECTION

1. Some faculty like to consult while others are more reluctant to discuss student situations with others (e.g., perception of their inadequacies or reluctance to cross boundaries). How comfortable are you with consulting with another faculty member or mental health professional about how to assist a student in distress?

2. Some faculty are more comfortable than others when discussing traumatic events and their consequences. What is your level of comfort with discussing traumatic events with others?

59

3. Be careful of the terms used when describing distressed students as many of the terms used are subject to misinformation, especially when used by those who do not have a background in mental health assessment. For example, the term and actual diagnosis of "bipolar" is one that is typically very misunderstood. How well do you understand the characteristics and effects of a diagnosis, other than hearing about them in informal conversations?

4. Excessive absences from class, particularly involving students who have not exhibited this pattern of behavior in the past, are often an indicator that a student may be experiencing some type of distress. How can you offer flexibility, within reason, for issues such as those mentioned in this narrative?

5. Dealing with stress is a very personal experience for most students. Some are very forthcoming regarding what they are dealing with in their lives, while others are more reserved. Based on your experiences, what are some of the reasons why students may not reach out when they are struggling with caring for loved ones?

NOTES

1. This figure is obtained by summing the disability-adjusted life years (DALYs) for both males and females in the age group 15 to 29 and dividing by the US population of 323,128,000 in 2016. Data on the US population was obtained from the Census Bureau.

2. "CMZ" is a fictitious acronym that is based on information associated with the student. None of this information is revealed in the narrative.

3. Over the semester, the number of absences accumulated by the student was equivalent to 30 percent of the class meetings.

REFERENCES

Hussain, R., Guppy, M., Robertson, S., & Temple, E. (2013). Physical and mental health perspectives of first year undergraduate rural university students. *BMC Public Health*, 13(1), 848. doi:10.1186/1471-2458-13-848

Mirowsky, J., & Ross, C. (2003). *Social causes of psychological distress*. New York, NY: Transaction Publishers.

National Institute of Mental Health (2019, February). *Mental illness*. Retrieved January 31, 2020, from www.nimh.nih.gov/health/statistics/mental-illness.shtml

Quesnel-Vallée, A., & Taylor, M. (2012). Socioeconomic pathways to depressive symptoms in adulthood: Evidence from the National Longitudinal Survey of Youth 1979. *Social Science & Medicine*, 74(5), 734–743. doi:10.1016/j.socscimed.2011.10.038

U.S. Department of Education. Institute of Education Sciences, National Center for Education Statistics (2018). *Digest of education statistics: 2018*. Retrieved from https://nces.ed.gov/programs/digest/d18/ (accessed January 11, 2020).

World Health Organization. (2018). *Global health estimates 2016: Disease burden by cause, age, sex, by country and by region, 2000–2016*. Geneva: Author.

World Health Organization (2019, October 23). *Adolescent mental health*. Retrieved from www.who.int/news-room/fact-sheets/detail/adolescent-mental-health

Chapter Four

Silent Grief and Invisible Presence

Toya Conston

I teach a personal and college success course at a four-year institution. This course is a lower-level undergraduate course that was developed for students to take in preparation for the remaining years of college in their respective degree programs, but mainly in their majors. In this class we explore topics such as time management, goal setting, how personal factors can impact academic outcomes, as well as how to cope with these challenges in order to reach degree attainment.

One semester I had what I will refer to as a "very special group." This group of students appeared very ambitious, anxious to learn and, while some of them were keenly aware of the content of the course, they were still attentive and attended each class meeting. This pattern was the flow at the beginning of the semester. Additionally, I was excited to teach and they were eager to learn—a perfect combination. As a primer in the course as the semester begins I always lead the class with the activity "My Story." I begin by telling students how I am not that far removed from the collegiate process (e.g., dealing with financial aid, working part-time jobs to make ends meet, experiencing setbacks) and that I was not the typical undergraduate student, as it took me seven years to earn my undergraduate degree. Based on my observations, I have found that facilitating this activity and sharing my story helps "normalize" the students' college experiences and encourages them to open up to me throughout the semester about the challenges they encounter. What I have observed over time is that every student has something they are going through, and some of those experiences can lead to distress.

For one of my assignments in the course, students are tasked with working together as a group and creating a presentation in which each of them will contribute one personal story and share advice with other students. Students are typically very apprehensive about the project initially; however, at the end of the assignment, they seem to feel empowered to share their stories. One student in particular began to share her story about how she learned to persevere even through sickness. In her story she talked about how she became very ill at the beginning of the semester (i.e., experiencing headaches, fatigue, nausea) and how the illness impacted her academic performance. Furthermore, she described how she was usually a studious student who stays on top of her assignments and gets good grades; but this semester was different. As an illustration of her diligence, she still attended class and participated in the group presentation because her group grade depended on her participation, in spite of appearing tired and depressed.

Later in the semester this student e-mailed me to request a meeting. The words of the email were unsettling to me as I perceived her anxiousness. She conveyed that she was very concerned about her grade in the course and wanted to discuss her progress. I obliged and scheduled a meeting the following week.

The student came to our scheduled meeting and began to ask questions about her status in the course. She expressed worry about her grades, how she felt very behind in the course, and did not believe she was doing well overall. After I reviewed her grades, she was only missing a couple of daily tasks due to missing class, but had submitted all major assignments. In fact, she was actually doing very well in the course and, even with some missed classes, she was on par to make a B or B+ in the course. In other words, she was not near failing, but was convinced she was.

After we discussed her status in the course, she seemed relieved and happy that she was not failing. I acknowledged that being sick could impact academic performance and I could understand why she was anxious about her grade in the course. At that moment she confessed that the sickness she was referring to in the presentation was actually a miscarriage.

She then shared how she had recently met a young man and they liked each other. She enjoyed spending time with him, but eventually concluded that they were not good for one another. Regrettably, she then found out she was pregnant by him, which caused an emotional struggle for her. The decision she made was to keep the baby a secret and only share news about the pregnancy with those in her most inner circle. While she knew that having a baby at this stage in her life would be hard, she had decided to keep the baby. She also knew that the boy was not someone with whom she saw a future, but was willing to have his baby for the sake of life. Unfortunately, she miscarried a few weeks later.

While she was sharing her story she held back her tears and I listened intently. Her sporadic attendance in the course made perfect sense to me now. The group assignment gave her a small outlet to express what she was feeling while disguising the secret and her distress. I consoled her as she talked and let her know how brave and proud I was that she was speaking

63

her truth out loud. I also shared how I understood loss and could only imagine what she was going through. Moreover, my goal was to first reassure her and then emphasize that her academic performance was related to the personal events going on in her life and she needed to acknowledge that fact.

Having previously studied the psychological effects of miscarriage and abortion, I understood some of the symptomology associated with such loss. With this understanding, I began to ask the student questions about other kinds of behavior she was engaging in such as substance or alcohol abuse, risk-taking behavior, and depression/anxiety. At that time she admitted that she was exhibiting all of the symptomology I mentioned—heavy drinking, which included going to happy hours almost every day of the week; engaging in risky sexual behavior; and feeling depressed and anxious. The student further explained that she was still participating in her daily activities such as school, work, and socializing with friends, but she did not feel present.

I shared with her that I believed the behavior she was exhibiting was associated with the loss of a child and, while I did not condone that behavior (because I wanted to make sure that I was not coming across as judgmental), I did want her to view her actions and reactions through a different lens. After additional discussion, I believe she was able to make the connection between her miscarriage and her behavior, which gave her a sense of ease and a better understanding of her feelings.

At the end of the meeting she apologized for sharing her story. I quickly reassured her that no apology was necessary and said how courageous she was to share her story with me. We hugged and she cried. I believe she gained a sense of relief from hugging another woman who could understand what she was going through. Furthermore, being her professor, I was someone whom she never thought would be a resource for her in such a personal time of grief. Moreover, I provided the student with campus resources if she wanted to talk with a qualified professional.

After our meeting, I chose to follow-up with the student and she was appreciative that I reached out. I plan to follow up with her as she continues to matriculate through the University. This student's story reaffirmed for me that students can endure things privately and oftentimes what they internalize is revealed through their academic outcomes.

I felt empowered to help this student in her time of need. Having an understanding of the psychological distress that a miscarriage can cause in addition to the impact distress can have on academic endeavors allowed me to express empathy for this student as she experienced grief. The University also encourages faculty to interact with, support, and create student engagement experiences to create a sense of community.

While I was not expecting this student to share such a personal experience with me, I felt I was well prepared to deal with the situation in a nonjudgmental manner and provide a source of comfort in her time of grief.

TAKEAWAYS

- A miscarriage and/or loss of an infant can be a very traumatic event in the life of an individual. In many instances the individual may show covert and/or overt symptoms of post-traumatic stress. It is important that everyone who deals with a student who is experiencing this kind of grief is sensitive to the impact it often has on their overall mental and emotional well-being.

- Misinterpreting a student's behavior or misreading their motivation can lead to an escalation in their distress level and precipitate unfortunate consequences.

- This narrative is a good example of how there can be a "deeper" reason for a student's behavior. In these instances, a private conversation with the affected student is almost always warranted.

- Please note how information was provided about the availability of counseling services, but the decision to take advantage of those services was left up to the student to consider and possibly pursue at a later time. If the student had been told she "needs therapy," she may not have been inclined to follow-up.

- It is important not to come across as judgmental and prescriptive. When conversing with a student in distress, the focus should remain on how their behavior is impacting their mental well-being as well as their daily functioning and progress. None of us really likes to feel we are being judged or chastised, and as soon as we feel personally challenged we tend to shift to a defensive mode and listening is minimal or nonexistent. Distressed students often need support—not criticism.

QUESTIONS FOR REFLECTION

1. If you had gone through a life event where you experienced feelings similar to what the student was describing, do you think this would have affected how you responded to the student? How? Similarly, if you could not relate to what she was describing, how might that lack of first-hand knowledge regarding how she might be feeling have affected your reaction?

2. Everyone tends to deal with personal loss differently. Grieving can be a very personal process that often plays out differently for

various individuals. How might the way you process the experience of loss interfere with your ability to be present and provide the kind of support the student needs in the present circumstance?

3. Genuine loss will occur in students' lives and it can be hard to have classroom policies that will assist those with legitimate grief and those who are just being manipulative and making up a loss or illness. How do you prefer to approach this challenge? What policies or rules do you have that allow you to make exceptions for some students? What policies or rules do you think should be put in place to provide guidance and support in these kinds of situations?

4. How do you feel about physical touch between you and a student? If you believe that it is okay to hug a student, are there exceptions to this?

5. How comfortable would you feel with addressing a student's personal choices and actions that you deemed detrimental and challenging to them?

Chapter Five

Setting Boundaries for Yourself When a Student is in Distress

Ryan Donovan

As an instructor and advisor in one of the largest majors at the university, I have the privilege of teaching and interacting with hundreds of students each semester. This fact, combined with my intentional efforts to be friendly, approachable, and empathetic in and out of the classroom, means that I am frequently approached by students in distress or by those who are concerned about their peers. While these situations vary widely in their cause and severity, one thing has become clear in recent years—students today are working increasingly hard to navigate and balance a new world of personal freedom with the anxiety of high academic expectations and the challenge of selecting a promising and meaningful professional path. When I remember this and combine it with my own experiences and challenges as an undergraduate student, I can make an enormous impact on those with whom I interact.

One recent situation stands out above most others. During the 2018 fall semester I was teaching a first-year health and wellness seminar course to approximately 100 students. This course focuses on the impact that individual behaviors and personal relationships have on physical, emotional, social, intellectual, spiritual, and financial well-being. Naturally, the course content leads to meaningful discussion of many of the issues new college students face—homesickness, anxiety, depression, disordered eating, substance abuse, etc. On one particular day, shortly after we had discussed healthy and unhealthy coping strategies for stress, a student came to my office during office hours. After a short conversation about how her classes were going, her career interests, and her family, she became visibly uneasy. She began to tremble as tears welled up in her eyes. After getting her a box of tissues and doing my best to reassure her that these reactions were common and nothing to be ashamed of, she began to open up regarding her current situation and state of mind.

What she described next was a combination of the challenges of being an out-of-state first-generation student with a history of anxiety and depression. She stated that the stresses of the transition to college and the first few weeks of class, combined with ongoing roommate conflicts, had significantly impacted her ability to sleep. She felt as if she "was in a downward spiral" regarding the dimensions of wellness we had been discussing in class. This was obviously concerning to me, though definitely not the first time a student has shared similar concerns in my office. I proceeded to ask her about her support network. She mentioned that she talked sporadically with her family and that they were aware that she was having some difficulty, but she had concealed the severity so as to not worry them. She also said that she had confided in one friend she has made since coming to campus, but, overall, she felt socially isolated. My first recommendation was for her to schedule an appointment with the Counseling Services office at our University Health Center.

All students receive several free counseling appointments with licensed psychologists who have an outstanding reputation (unfortunately, this means that students frequently must wait weeks to get an appointment). She responded that she had been to therapy before and that she "would look into it." Because I did not determine that she was in imminent danger, I believed this was a positive next step. Before concluding our meeting, I asked if she would mind if I followed-up with her on a regular basis, simply to check-in and see if there was anything I could do to offer support. She agreed that would be good and promised to reach out again if her situation changed. Overall, I felt optimistic that she would weather this challenging time successfully by leaning on the people (including me) and the resources available to her.

Approximately one week later, this student's closest friend approached me after class and asked me if we could meet. Though I did not have scheduled office hours at that time, I always strive to make myself available to all students whenever possible. We made small talk as we walked to my office, but once we arrived she wasted no time in expressing her concern for her friend. She described a pattern of self-deprecating comments and actions. Her friend had been drinking regularly and had isolated herself from nearly everyone on her residence hall floor. She had also described a history of injurious behaviors including disordered eating and cutting throughout her time in high school. This student continued to explain how these actions were beginning to take a negative toll on her. She wanted to be supportive but did not know what else she could do. Though I did not divulge that I had already met with her friend, I encouraged her to continue to be supportive and said that I would reach out directly to her friend. Finally, I asked that she continue to take care of herself and her own wellness, emphasizing that she could not be there for her friend if she did not maintain her own sense of physical, emotional, and social well-being.

Following this conversation, I made regular contact with the student in distress. I sent her emails approximately every week and went out of my way to make friendly conversation with her before and after class. Throughout the next several weeks, she repeatedly stated that she was "doing well" and that she had made an appointment with (though not yet seen) a counselor. Her demeanor did seem to be improved, and her class attendance and academic performance was satisfactory. All-in-all, I interpreted this information positively and did not see any reason for further intervention.

As stated previously, these situations are not uncommon, particularly when I teach first-semester freshmen. What made this particular case unique was what happened next. During the first weekend in October my wife and I were away from campus for a weekend to celebrate our anniversary. Though I do my best to disconnect from work while on vacation, I don't always succeed. This was one time that rule exception turned out to be good. As I was waiting for my wife to get ready to go to dinner on Saturday night, I briefly checked my email. Among other non-urgent messages, I had received a note from the friend of the student I had been concerned about. In the email, sent only 15 minutes before I had checked my phone, she said that her friend was intoxicated and talking about cutting herself. The concerned friend also mentioned that she was contemplating taking an entire bottle of sleeping pills that "she wasn't even supposed to have." The friend said she was worried, scared, and did not know what to do. I knew immediately that I had to intervene. Being seven hours away, I was limited on the actions I could take. I replied to the email quickly, asking her to stay with her friend and that I was going to reach out to the appropriate professionals who could assist.

Moreover, I texted a colleague who was in town and knew of this student's history and current struggles. She was able to provide me with the phone number of the student's resident hall assistant (RA). I called her RA, stated my concern, and asked that she seek out the student immediately to ensure her safety. Her response was one of reluctance and she said she would "find the residence hall director." Unsatisfied with this plan, I called the university's support and safety assessment hotline. After leaving a message, I finally received a call back from a counselor nearly an hour later asking for more details about the student and the current situation. I was assured that they would "follow-up" with the student and the residence hall director. This conversation ended with me feeling uneasy and nervous for the student. At the same time, I knew that I had taken the appropriate action and had to trust in the process that I had set in motion. I wondered if I should do more. Simultaneously, I wanted and needed to respect my wife and our relationship that we were away celebrating.

I did not receive any follow-up information that night or the next morning. Because I wanted to be sure that my student was safe and receiving the help she needed, I called and left a message with the residence hall director on Sunday afternoon. It was early evening before he returned my call, but he did assure me that she was doing better today and that her RA was checking in with her frequently. With that comfort, I decided that I had a duty to reach out to the student directly. Because I did not have her personal phone number, I sent a brief email letting her know that I had been made aware of her situation the night before and, therefore, had an obligation to reach out to offer help. More importantly, I emphasized that it was not just out of professional obligation, but because I genuinely cared about her well-being. I asked if she would be interested in meeting again during the next week. In her follow-up email the next morning she said that she was "okay" and that she "was just going to focus on her classes" and would let me know if she wanted to meet. While this was not the response I was hoping for, I respected the student's request for privacy and trusted that I would hear from her or her friend if anything changed. I did maintain cordial communications with the student throughout the remainder of the semester, sending her emails and chatting before or after class. She never returned to my office, and I was saddened to learn that she withdrew from the university after the semester.

Students attend institutions of higher education to prepare themselves for the rest of their lives. For many, this means studying and learning concepts that will help them secure rewarding professional careers. I, however, believe that the growth that occurs along the way is much more valuable. This growth has little to do with content knowledge and more to do with self-awareness and personal development. I can only hope that my contribution to this growth is as significant and meaningful as what's on the next exam.

TAKEAWAYS

- While we all strive to protect a student's privacy, there are times when it is appropriate and necessary to involve other campus personnel. When a faculty has reason to believe a student may be at imminent risk of self-harm or harming others, it is appropriate to reach out to the Dean of Students (who is often a part of a campus safety team or risk assessment/intervention team, if applicable to your campus). Additionally, Residence Hall staff are often asked to do welfare or safety checks on students and a Resident Assistant will almost always defer to a Hall Director. Generally speaking, we would rather defend our actions if a complaint is made about violating privacy than have to defend taking no action when a student harms themselves.

■ In this situation, the faculty member could also seek support and advice from the university counseling center. Counseling centers will not share information about their clients, but they will take in any information that might concern a client. It is always advisable to consult with those who have the experience and expertise in dealing with these kinds of students. They will be able to provide insights and potential strategies that the average faculty member may not have thought about or used.

■ Many students in higher education today are struggling as they are balancing academic, financial, social, and personal stressors. Although some of their challenges are the same ones many faculty experienced as undergraduate students, other challenges are very different. It is important for those in positions of trust to recognize this and do their best to learn and adapt to changing student characteristics. Faculty members often have the opportunity to break down barriers and dispel stereotypes and myths each day in the classroom. One way this can be accomplished is by faculty sharing their own stories and struggles as college students (at an appropriate level) and how they overcame them, especially if they reached out to others for assistance, or to articulate that they understand the struggles of college life. Students need to see faculty as real people with real lives outside of academia. Being a bit vulnerable is one way to do this.

■ A small percentage of students who are distressed have a history of avoiding professional treatment and, instead, rely on a select few to be their support. We understand the reluctance to seek professional therapy, but we do not want to enable this approach. This small percentage may be vacillating between a sincere desire for help and a more manipulative call for attention. It is okay to mix firmness with empathy.

■ Faculty must come to terms with the fact that they cannot "fix" every challenge faced by every student who walks into their office. They should do their best to listen empathetically and connect students in distress to whatever resources are available. There are trained counselors to serve as a resource and faculty should not be expected to conduct themselves as trained counselors. Sometimes, as illustrated in this narrative, students will decide to leave the institution. This outcome is not a failure on the part of the faculty member.

71

- Research has shown that having a support system has many positive benefits, including a reduction in stress, depression, and anxiety. Asking a student in distress if they have a support system is a good query because it helps to ascertain to whom, if anyone, they can reach out for help.
- When a student provides evidence that s/he is contemplating suicide, it is a common response to become alarmed. Upon encountering such a student in distress, we may notice our pulse rates increase, our skin becoming flush and hot, our stomach churning, and a sense of going into fight, flight, or freeze. All of these are normal responses and are understood as "secondary trauma." Rather than waiting until such an encounter, prepare yourself now.

QUESTIONS FOR REFLECTION

1. Imagine yourself getting the phone call that this author received. What initial cognitive, emotional, and physiological responses might you feel? How will you self-soothe yourself so as to slow down your thought process, manage your heart rate, and ground yourself?
2. The Dean of Students and/or the counseling center staff are scheduled to speak to faculty in your department about engaging distressed students. If you attended this meeting, what questions would you have for these professionals? What questions do you think they might have for you?
3. Technology continues to play an increasing role in situations involving students in distress. Is it appropriate to communicate with students in these and similar situations via texting, e-mail, and social media? Why or why not? What are some reasonable expectations for communicating with colleagues about students who are in distress? When would these kinds of ways of communication become inappropriate?
4. How would you approach a situation in which a peer or friend of a distressed student comes to you to express concern?
5. What are your particular beliefs about the limits of responsibility and boundaries for helping a student in distress?

Chapter Six

The Case of the Senior Citizen Student

Christopher L. Giroir

Higher education has seen an influx of all types of students, including non-traditional senior citizens returning to the classroom to pursue their educational goals. As a faculty member in a graduate program, it is not uncommon to see more "seasoned" individuals in classes; however, adding a 70-year-old student did bring a new dynamic to class discussions and the student cohort. Our institution created a tuition and fee waiver for senior citizens (individuals over the age of 65) in an effort to build a positive relationship with the local community and to bring a more diverse population to the campus. The tuition-free program was not originally intended for students to pursue a degree; however, there were no restrictions preventing them from earning either a Bachelor's or a graduate degree.

Being one of the largest graduate programs at the institution, it was not uncommon to see a diverse number of candidates apply for admission each academic year. The graduate program welcomes students in the traditional classroom where technology often complements instruction or students can pursue the degree entirely online. In this particular case, the senior citizen student decided to pursue the bricks-and-mortar route in the traditional classroom with a cohort of students, mostly holding graduate assistantships. Students were originally receptive to the input from our newest student, a White 70-year-old female who had dreams of pursuing a graduate degree for her "bucket list" goal of earning an advanced degree.

As the semester progressed, it became clear that the non-traditional senior citizen student was one who sought out attention. In class discussions she always had to contribute to the conversation, even if her comments were not necessarily germane to the subject being discussed. Her contributions were often random and non-coherent, which quickly led to a disgruntled cohort of classmates who often became disengaged and non-receptive to her observations. The body language and non-verbal messages being sent from her classmates to the senior citizen student were clear and, consequently, the tension she generated could be felt throughout the classroom. In addition to adding random comments, she would also stand up and walk around the room because various health conditions prevented her from sitting for extended periods of time. This pacing would lead many students to become distracted and the focus would often shift from a relatively lively and engaging discussion to simply watching the senior citizen student walking around the room.

In administering the course, I would place the class assignments, required readings, and lecture PowerPoint presentations on the online learning platform used by our institution. Students would log into the platform to access this information as well as to submit their completed work for evaluation. Instructions were provided in the syllabus on how to access the online components of the course and how to upload to their completed assignments. The senior citizen student struggled with technology and did not submit any of her work electronically as instructed, claiming that she did not understand how to use the platform. Instead of submitting her assignments electronically as requested, she would bring her assignments to class and hand them to me, always complaining that she simply did not understand how to use her computer. She would also repeatedly ask questions in class regarding how to use technology and constantly shared with everyone in the class that her computer did not work properly.

In the class, students often would engage in small group discussions in order to dissect complex issues. As part of this process, groups would self-select members, often leaving the senior citizen student alone, sending an unmistakable message to her that she was not welcome. At the same time, the senior citizen student initially seemed to be challenged when it came to reading social cues; consequently, she would often invite herself into groups where she was clearly not wanted. Eventually, she began to notice that she was being cut-off in conversations and began to confront others in an inappropriate manner. Several members of the class were singled out by the senior citizen student and accused of not being inclusive and discriminating against her based on her age. This accusation usually forced the other students to deny these claims and invite the senior citizen student into their group. Moreover, when the other students in the class began to avoid seeking her input, the senior citizen student would often appear to have some type of medical issue such as a migraine, light-headedness, stomach-ache, hot flashes, etc. It should also be noted that she was overly descriptive and explicit in her descriptions of these health issues and usually addressed the class as a whole during these episodes.

As the instructor for the course, I invited the senior citizen student to come speak with me about her true intention for pursuing a graduate degree and about her behavior in the class. During this conversation, she stated she did not realize she was causing any kind of disruption—even after specific and detailed examples were shared with her. Further, she indicated that she was going to make a conscious effort not to cause any disruptions going forward. The disruptive behavior, however, continued to be manifested after our discussion. Subsequently, I shared the experience I was having with the senior citizen student with my faculty colleagues. I wanted to see if the conduct I was observing was limited to my class or if they were witnessing the same behavior in their classes. After a brief consultation we determined the behavior was relatively consistent and, in some cases, even more problematic than I had encountered.

After the conversation with my colleagues, I determined that I needed to seek additional assistance and support in order to address the challenges most of the faculty seemed to be experiencing with the senior citizen student. Since I served as department chair, I decided to consult with the academic Dean of the college on how to best intervene with the student. The meeting was inconclusive (and somewhat frustrating) with the academic Dean advising me to proceed cautiously as we did not want to violate the student's rights and potentially invite a harassment lawsuit involving age discrimination. Our institution was fortunate to have a student intervention team, which was housed within the Division of Student Affairs that worked with students who were exhibiting challenges. After basically getting no support from the Dean, I submitted a request to the student intervention team related to the senior citizen student. A team member from the campus counseling center subsequently contacted me after reviewing my request and indicated that the intervention team planned to invite the student in for a discussion about her behavior in all of her graduate courses.

Long story short, I did not see any changes in the senior citizen student's behavior, attitude, or demeanor even after she supposedly met with the student intervention team. As I continued to teach the graduate course, I began to notice other students on the course voicing their displeasure with the constant disruptions by the senior citizen student. Eventually they called for her to be removed from the class as she was having an increasingly detrimental impact on the learning environment. I reminded them of how, at the beginning of the course, we discussed how in the proverbial "real world" we often are required to work with people who we perceive to be difficult and challenging. As the course progressed, however, I could sense that this rationalization was no longer appeasing the students in the class and that frustration was growing with the senior citizen student. These students frequently reminded me that they have rights as well and felt no one was listening to their concerns. In sum, they thought I was going too far to accommodate the senior citizen student to the detriment of the rest of the class. I tried to reassure the students that I was acutely aware of the issues and that I was working to address them as effectively and as fairly as I could. But, to be completely transparent, I was also becoming very frustrated as well. I had the sense that no one at the institution was taking the situation seriously and no one was really even interested in addressing the matter. Certainly, I was not getting any support or guidance on how to handle the situation.

Since the situation with the senior citizen student seemed to be getting worse, I again reached out to her, but this time I took a somewhat different approach. Since she had shared with me (as well as the rest of the class) on numerous occasions that she had some fairly serious health challenges, I reiterated that she might want to seek assistance from the Office of Disability Accommodations. I suggested there could be some special accommodations made that could help her to be more successful in not only my class, but in her other graduate classes as well. I hoped that by requesting an accommodation, this would provide me with an opportunity to speak with the professionals in that office about her disruptive behaviors and to see if they had any ideas on how to better approach the deteriorating classroom environment I was experiencing. The senior citizen student seemed to appreciate the conversation and concern I had expressed for her and stated she would take that option under consideration. Ultimately, she felt that she was not "handicapped" and therefore did not need any "special help." Obviously, this latest attempt to address her behavior did not go as planned and, once again, I was at a loss for how to deal with her disruptive behavior.

As the semester continued to progress, the senior citizen's disruptive behaviors persisted, although I slowly began to be more proactive in cutting off the seemingly random thoughts that were being shared much more expediently than I had been doing earlier in the term. Students on the course also began to become much more aggressive and vocal with their reactions, often talking over and essentially ignoring the student when her comments were not perceived to be relevant to the discussion at hand. When this began to occur on a consistent basis, I became extremely frustrated. I knew the other students were losing their patience with the senior citizen student. Moreover, having students talk over each other in class is disrespectful and counterproductive to the educational experience. Students cannot learn when they are uncomfortable and distressed.

My last resort was to reach out to the Dean of Students to see if there was any assistance that office could provide to help me deal with a situation that was growing worse with each class meeting. Initially, I did not know if the Dean was willing to intervene with a classroom-related issue as their office primarily deals with student conduct and other issues that are traditionally considered outside of the classroom. The Dean wanted to know what steps I had taken in an attempt to address disruptive behaviors exhibited by the senior citizen student. I provided an overview of everything that had transpired up to that point. The Dean told me the senior citizen student would be contacted and asked to schedule a meeting with their office in order to discuss the situation. Apparently, her disruptive behavior could be interpreted as a possible violation of the Code of Student Conduct.

After her meeting with the Dean of Students had taken place, the senior citizen student returned to class. When class was over, she indicated that she wanted to speak with me about that encounter. She was very angry that I referred her to the Dean of Students and she let me know that she did not appreciate the university "threatening to kick a senior citizen out of the institution." I tried to explain to her that her age was not the issue and that the entire concern was related to her disruptive behavior and its impact on the other students. I shared how I, along with her classmates, were appreciative of her life experiences and wanted to hear about them—as long as they were relevant to the class discussion we were having at the moment. I also reassured her that no one was trying to "kick her out" of the class, the program, or the institution; it was simply that her behavior was perceived to be extremely disruptive and, as such, was negatively impacting the learning environment for the other students enrolled in the class. Interestingly, the senior citizen student did not seem to be able to recall the numerous meetings we had in which this concern was discussed and she was informed that her disruptive behavior was not acceptable. I explained that since she did not seem able to control her behavior even after multiple conversations, I felt I had to get others at the institution involved for the benefit of the class as a whole. Again, she responded that she felt disrespected by my chosen course of action and that she felt that she was not welcome at the institution. After this last exchange, the senior citizen student decided to withdraw for the university; she did not return the following semester.

As noted, this situation was only resolved when the senior citizen student voluntarily removed herself from the situation. My concern, in addition to losing a student who genuinely wanted to continue her education, revolves around the lingering notion that there should have been more options available to me as a faculty member. Moreover, I am confident this type of scenario is not an isolated occurrence. Given the millions of students in higher education, it no doubt plays out in one form or another on a fairly regular basis. As a faculty member who constantly strives to do the proverbial "right thing," I came to the realization that I was not prepared in my academic program to deal with challenges posed by distressed students. I was fortunate to transition into the faculty role after spending several years as a student affairs professional, primarily in the area of housing and residence life. In that role, we faced difficult and disruptive students/parents on a regular basis and I was trained in how to deal with those kinds of situations in an effective, efficient, and balanced manner. In my present position, however, it was discouraging to discover that there were no clear steps outlined for faculty to follow when faced with "challenging" students, including when they are causing distress among other students. Consequently, many faculty feel they simply have to tolerate bad behaviors because they do not feel they will be supported by administrators if they attempt to resolve the situation on their own. They are simply not given viable intervention options.

I think it is important to point out that attention-seeking behaviors are not necessarily the exclusive domain of younger, less-mature individuals, as illustrated by the present case study. Anyone can engage in these kinds of counterproductive behaviors, but I think the circumstances under which they tend to occur are somewhat universal, i.e., when a student is significantly older than the instructor. Like many in my generation, I was raised to respect my elders. In retrospect, I believe this attitude and disposition may have contributed to me tolerating the situation for much longer than I should have. For the good of everyone involved, however, faculty must maintain a clear and unambiguous focus on providing a positive learning environment for all students. As such, I feel like I let my students down in the way I chose to deal with the senior citizen student.

Finally, in relation to the situation I just described, my direct supervisor could not provide any insights or suggestions regarding how to proceed, and seemed more concerned about avoiding a lawsuit than with resolving my classroom imbroglio. Keep in mind that, from my vantage point, the biggest challenge was not my inability to manage the classroom environment; rather, it was the other students in the class who were adversely affected by the attention-seeking behaviors of a lone student. This situation also played out during the course of an entire semester, which I believe is much too long. As these situations arise in the future, it is important for the university community to make sure avenues are in place for students, staff, and faculty to be able to share the challenges they encounter and be provided with concrete strategies for intervening appropriately and effectively.

TAKEAWAYS

- Most faculty have not had training or formal education in human growth and development; as such, they are not well-versed in the dynamics that may be occurring in situations like those described above. This narrative underscores the importance of having a basic understanding of the needs and desires, as well as the organic issues associated with someone who is aging. It is important to invest in learning more about all the diversity and cultural dynamics of students, including various age groups, and the associated challenges in and out of the classroom.

- When disruptive behavior in the classroom is causing distress for others, it is important to deal with these kinds of situations on a continuum that begins with having a brief meeting to mention the disruptive nature of the behaviors being exhibited and then progresses to more serious interventions if the desired outcome is not achieved (i.e., if the inappropriate and disruptive behaviors continue). Note how the faculty member first held a private meeting with the student and was open, honest, and direct about their concerns. A lack of response from the student then set the stage for taking the matter further. In some cases, faculty (and administrators/staff) get more people involved—typically at higher levels—before seriously attempting to address the situation themselves. This is not good practice.

- Note how the faculty member consulted with peers about the senior citizen student's disruptive behavior. Consultation is a critical step when attempting to address situations such as the one described. It is important to know if other faculty are experiencing the same behavior or if this is a more isolated occurrence. Obviously, if the behavior is limited to the one faculty member's classes, it will need to be approached in a different manner than if the behavior is somewhat uniform across classes.

- This is an excellent example of how vital it is for faculty to familiarize themselves with the institutional code of conduct. Psychological disorders, personality styles, and cultural differences can be appreciated, but they do not absolve a student from the responsibility they have to adhere to established parameters of appropriate behavior on a college campus. Many higher education administrators have shared the idea that we have to deal primarily with overt behavior—not underlying motives, reasons, or intentions, etc. Those factors are relevant although there are standards of conduct, including classroom behaviors, that are required of students regardless of their personal characteristics.

- When a student or a small number of students is causing distress for their peers in the classroom, it is best to not ignore the situation. Take steps to address it immediately and efficiently; document all behaviors and your efforts; and focus on the classroom environment for those negatively impacted. Of course, even when you take steps to prevent disruptive behavior in the classroom, you cannot guarantee a disruption-free class and how it can impact the other students.

QUESTIONS FOR REFLECTION

1. What do you feel was the core issue in the case of the senior citizen student? If you had to assess responsibility for the events as they unfolded, who would you hold most accountable for this unfortunate situation? Make a strong case for your conclusions.

2. In dealing with these kinds of situations, the approach must be two-fold. First, corrective steps must be taken to deal with the immediate behaviors on display as well as their consequences, both intended and unintended. Second, preventative steps must be implemented to lessen the probability that these behaviors will be exhibited in the future. Please identify and explain at least three interventions that should be taken in the short-term (corrective) as well as three changes that need to be implemented on a more long-term basis (preventative)?

3. What is your reaction to the lack of support provided to the faculty member by other members of the academic community (his supervisor, the dean, the student intervention team)? Do you feel this is fairly common on today's college campuses? How does this lack of support impact the faculty member's ability to perform the duties and responsibilities associated with their role as a faculty member? What should each of these parties have done when made aware of the situation by the faculty member?

4. Reflect on your own biases and prejudices (and we all have them). What assumptions do you, or have you, made about students who are older than yourself? Younger than yourself? The same age as yourself? Has this awareness altered your perspective and actions when you are engaging in classroom discussions and assignments?

5. The author speaks to the importance of balancing a positive learning environment while also being respectful and understanding of students who may be unintentionally causing disruption. What were your initial thoughts as you read this narrative? What could the faculty member have done differently to deal with the situation? What would you consider to be an ideal outcome of the semester-long episode?

6. Sometimes distressed students tend to be disruptive students (but not always) and often conduct issues must be addressed before or concurrently with any psychological or emotional challenge. As such, counseling can be a very effective intervention for distressed students—but it has a limited effect on students who do not want to engage in the process. Moreover, counseling should never be used to "fix" disruptive students. What is your understanding of how counseling works? Does your university's counseling center offer a program or workshop for faculty (or a local agency for campuses with counseling centers) on the services they provide?

Chapter Seven

Feeling the Pressure When Facing the Unexpected

Lia Howard

In this chapter I will discuss two situations—one in which I had to engage with a student in distress due to an upsetting choice they had to make and another in which I had to reach out to a student service to ensure there were proper resources available for a student in transition. In both situations I learned valuable things about myself and came out of the situations with more knowledge than when I went into them.

SITUATION #1

I spent one semester visibly pregnant. As a point of reference, I ended up going into labor hours after submitting my grades that semester. One day midway through the semester, one of my female students in a large lecture course came to my office hours. She was upset and had been crying. She began her sentence, "I need to tell you something but only two other people know." Immediately I felt uncomfortable. I told her, "While I am happy to talk with you, our counseling office is better equipped than I am to help you." She tearily nodded but continued, "I want to talk with you."

She then proceeded to tell me that she was pregnant and that her mother, who was paying her tuition, told her that she would stop paying for her classes unless she got an abortion. She had three days to do so or her mom would immediately stop all tuition payments.

Again, I felt uncomfortable. I was in a tough position. The institution was a private, sectarian university that had a position on abortion aligned with its larger religious affiliation (fine print: it was against abortion). I had no idea what she was inferring about my own views. Was she opening up to me because she could see I was pregnant and, thus, she was guessing that I would be sympathetic to her situation? I hoped she would have known from the way I teach that I am pro-woman; but I could only guess what she was thinking about me beyond the fact that I too (though married and a decade plus older) was pregnant. At the same time, I was well aware that, not being trained as a psychologist, I lacked the correct tools to best affirm her while allowing her own voice to emerge. I felt caught in a situation that I was not best equipped to handle and felt under pressure to answer my student the "right way."

In terms of the specifics of her situation, multiple things were going on and I tried to compose my face as I ticked through these things in my mind. First, her mother was using tuition as the means by which to compel her daughter to make a choice that seemed to be against the student's wishes. Second, there was not a lot of time for her to comply with her mother's deadline. Third (and most importantly), as her professor, I had absolutely no say in the matter. My views on abortion and family, though tempting to incorporate, were not being asked for and would only further complicate this already complicated situation.

I decided that it would be best for me to direct her to all of the places on campus that would help her. Counseling and Psychological Services seemed like an obvious place to reference. After that, however, I began to draw a blank. I was relatively new to the institution, so I was unaware of the full menu of resources available to her. I had no idea, for example, if her mother stopped paying tuition effective that week, whether the student would be permitted to finish the semester and remain in my class. I did not know if the university had a way to support traditional undergraduate students with children. Regardless, I did not want my lack of knowledge to inform her decision. I did not want her to feel like I was pushing her in one direction simply because I did not know if she would be supported in the other direction by the institution (though it has a public position on abortion, I had no idea if it had programmatic commitments that would support student mothers).

The tricky part was that our class had deadlines as well and, while I could understand the immediacy of her situation and the real pressures she was under, the only thing I had any jurisdiction over was my course. I could offer extensions but that seemed like such a shallow comfort to offer as she navigated this intense life event.

I looked at her and said that I was grateful that she reached out to me. I told her that this was an important choice that she needed to make on her own regardless of all of the external voices she may be hearing. I suggested that she make her decision an informed decision—that she research the possibilities available to her and think about them. I told her that, with her permission, I would connect her to our Office of Student Success for a consultation and that they would be able to refer her to all of the additional resources on campus that could help her.

Further, I told her that I would be happy to work with her to develop a plan for success in my course. I told her she could take a rescheduled version of our exam after she made her decision. As we talked, I made it clear to her that since I was teaching many classes that semester, I would need to make sure it was scheduled in advance so that it did not become an administrative detail that got lost in my scheduling. She seemed to understand and left my office.

My course met three times a week that semester, so she came to check in with me once more after class that week but, after that brief talk, she stopped communicating with me about personal things. I checked in with the Office of Student Success to make sure she met with them and to make sure she was on their radar; but I did not feel comfortable asking her any follow up questions beyond a general, "How are you doing?"

The entire situation was very overwhelming for me. I felt caught by surprise and out of my depth in terms of the help I could offer her. My office hours are generally routine moments where students ask for help on essays, theoretical concepts, or incorrect test answers, and I am able to provide them quite quickly with comprehensive solutions to their questions. This was a problem that I could not solve. The intense personal nature of the student's issue, the fact that the issue is divisive and laced with moral judgment, and the fact that I too was pregnant added to my discomfort in terms of checking in with the student to see what she decided or to see how she was coping with whatever decision she decided on. It is a situation that to this day is still not resolved in my mind, though I am not sure I could have handled it any other way.

SITUATION #2

I was teaching a large lecture class—an introductory class within my discipline that many non-majors took to fulfill other requirements. One evening I received an email from a student saying that he was transitioning to a woman. He asked that I no longer call him by his former name and asked that I use feminine pronouns when talking about him and call him by his new name from this point forward. I emailed back indicating that of course I would change the pronouns and the name in my grade book. I asked the student to further let me know if there was anything else I could do to make her time in my class smooth during this process.

The next day the student walked into class wearing a long blond curly costume-style wig that went almost to her waist. It was tangled and looked askew. Additionally, the student's outfit was attention grabbing—bold colors and a short mini skirt with multi-colored tights. She had (understandably) inexpertly applied lipstick so that it was smeared over parts of her lower face. The general effect was arresting and my first thought was "fraternity prank." It was quickly followed by genuine concern that my other students would laugh or bestow unwanted attention on this student.

Lecturing was more difficult that day as I scanned the class and tried to maintain a welcoming, safe, affirming face as I taught my material. Yet, each time I turned to the transitioning student's section of the classroom, I was surprised anew by her look. To my great relief, none of the students in that large auditorium seemed phased by the transitioning student and the class finished without a hitch. The student did not decide to meet with me after class.

The next class the student added large sparkly sunglasses to the outfit and, over the course of the next few classes, additional accessories were added that were equally bold fashion choices relative to the dressing habits of the rest of the class. The campus unwritten dress code vacillates between a more preppy style to wearing exercise clothes or pajamas, but all are often in muted colors. Many of the students attended high schools with uniforms and some of the faculty in our department joked about the informal uniform of campus. My transitioning student was not following any of the informal uniform cues. She was making other fashion choices.

I was concerned for my student. Each class, I was nervous that she would be teased for her unkempt hair or smeared lipstick or bold fashion choices. Yet, I wanted to affirm the student in her transition and experimentation with different ways of expressing herself. I was also worried that older faculty might not be kind to the student as she transitioned. Our university, up to that point, had a limited number of students who had transitioned; so faculty (myself included) did not have as much exposure to this population as some other university environments. I did not want this particular student to feel in any way stigmatized or exoticized while in transition.

I reached out to our Assistant Vice President in our Office of Student Success for a meeting. In her office I shared my concern that the university was perhaps not doing its best in supporting students who were transitioning as their process might be misperceived by other students as fraternity pranks. Together we discussed ways of helping students, offering opportunities to connect with the fashion and beauty club or other types of opportunities that would help students like mine get added practice in looking pulled together and professional as they made the transition.

The rest of the semester went smoothly and I did not have much one-on-one interaction with the student. She seemed to settle into a more established look that drew less attention. I had absolutely no training in how to handle a situation like that—not even an email announcement from the university or an article from the *Chronicle of Higher Education*—so, again, I am not sure if I did it the "right way." I felt good about reaching out to my university's Office of Student Success and was deeply reassured that I had a

85

community within the administration, most particularly the Assistant Vice President of Student Success, who cared about me and about students. She was receptive, helpful, and collaborative and that felt very good.

CONCLUDING THOUGHTS

In conclusion, both situations, and several others that I have experienced since, have caught me unawares and unprepared. In office hours I have had students share with me that they were raped, that a parent is dying or is very sick, that they struggle with depression/anxiety, and that they are food insecure. I have found myself floundering and then calling our Office of Student Success. I did this so frequently in my first couple of years at my institution that the Assistant Vice President of Student Success asked me to start presenting with her at faculty workshops. What I found interesting while presenting is that not every faculty member has students who share these stories with them. Several older male faculty had been teaching for decades at my institution and had not heard any stories like the ones I was sharing during our workshop.

TAKEAWAYS (SITUATION #1)

- This is an excellent example of a situation that includes not only a physical and academic crisis, but also a moral and spiritual one. In reality, most encounters are multi-layered and more complicated than is often assumed in the beginning. The latter can often be very difficult to process and sift through even when we are not in crisis. Offering a non-judgmental open ear along with directing the student to referral sources (on-campus resources, spiritual mentor) will go a much longer way than giving advice.
- This narrative is also an excellent example of how quickly we can feel overwhelmed and worry about doing the right thing. Remember that a life crisis usually takes time and a process to solve. Faculty can be very helpful as part of the "start" to the process; they do not have to "fix" the whole situation for a student. This faculty member did very well to provide empathy, encouragement, and to recommend additional services, like counseling and a visit with financial aid. More times than not, students have an interesting way of choosing who they will involve in their process. Often, students are "testing the water," and they are willing to seek counseling after they are heard and understood by faculty.
- As noted, this situation includes not only a physical and academic crisis, but a moral and spiritual one as well. The latter can often

be very difficult to process and sift through even when we are not in crisis. Offering a non-judgmental open ear along with directing the student to referral sources (e.g., on-campus resources, spiritual mentor) is much more important—and much more effective—than simply giving advice.

QUESTIONS FOR REFLECTION

1. Offering opinions in crisis situations typically adds more pressure on the student rather than actually helping them. How will you refrain from giving opinions, especially if that is something you are used to doing?
2. Sometimes students will present the faculty member with a situation that may involve an issue that the instructor has strong feelings about, either positively or negatively. If a student comes to you with an issue that is a "hot button" or "touchy" topic for you, what strategies will you use to set aside what you believe and assist them in a non-judgmental way?
3. Some issues students present to you could be unsettling and impact your disposition. What are some strategies you undertake when you need to decompress and maintain your personal well-being?

TAKEAWAYS (SITUATION #2)

- While this is not necessarily the presenting issue in the case provided, let's consider an experience with a student who came to class disheveled and not showered. Her hygiene is also very poor. Often our first impulse may be to disengage, stay away, and even view the individual with disgust. However, more often than not, poor hygiene is not necessarily the individual's preferred choice. They may be homeless. They may only have one change of clothes and limited access to washing machines. They may be clinically depressed. They also may remain in dirty clothes so as to keep their sexual abuser away. We may never know the situation, however there is always a context.
- Sometimes the student has not expressed distress when informing you about a life change, but the faculty member may feel unprepared in situations with which they are unfamiliar and about which they have limited knowledge. Reaching out to professionals in student service departments who have been trained to work with students in distress and knowing where the resources are to assist them can be an asset for a faculty member. As in this narrative, the faculty

reached out for support, which is always a good choice in those moments of uncertainty.

■ Some faculty are approachable and students feel comfortable talking to them. This perception could put those faculty members in a position of consistently being sought out for support during moments of distress. What can be an unfortunate consequence is that these faculty can become worn out by being in so many support systems, especially in light of the many other duties and expectations faculty must tackle.

QUESTIONS FOR REFLECTION

1. Again, offering opinions in crisis situations typically adds to the anxiety that the student is already experiencing (i.e., it can be very counterproductive). How will you refrain from giving opinions, especially if that is something you are used to doing?

2. The line between what is acceptable and what is not often evolves. The probability that someone will misinterpret your comments always exists and no one wants to be accused of impropriety when they are simply trying to help. How will you navigate the sensitive nature of improper dress and/or make-up so that your intervention is sensitive and will not come across as harassment?

3. A faculty member's life is deceptively complex and time-consuming. Students know which instructors are more available/approachable and, consequently, tend to seek them out on a more consistent basis. What are your thoughts about faculty who are more approachable and sought out by students in moments of distress having to direct some of their time from other tasks, such as teaching, service, or research, to help students?

Chapter Eight

When Identity Issues and Cultural Foundations Cause Distress

It Takes Time

Trish Lindsey Jaggers

My chest clinched as I read a student's essay. I struggled to maintain composure through the closing paragraphs of a narrative whose author spent several pages celebrating a long-awaited pregnancy only to discover, at the end of her pregnancy, that her baby suffers from a bone disease so horrific its bones (chest, legs, arms) are crushed during removal through the C-section. Her final paragraph details the choice she and her husband must now make: maintain life support for a few months (if that) of excruciating suffering for this newborn they love or allow her to die. They choose the latter.

As a writing instructor, I've long known that most every student has an internal wound to tend, a particularly difficult obstacle or issue they've overcome, and seldom does any opportunity present itself for them to discuss, analyze, and mend that wound before it scars over, still tender. Few college assignments invite students to divulge personal information the way a personal narrative essay does. Personal writing, when students know it will be shared with no one other than their professor, becomes their totem of expression, and, simultaneously, their chance to heal. Consequently, I've had Pandora's Box opened and presented to me, and on more than one occasion, I've had my breath taken.

Out of those occasions, two rise to the surface. During those periods, my particular department (Academic Support) served academically underprepared students—students admitted to the university with deficiencies in English composition, literacy, and/or mathematics. (It was not uncommon for students to have deficiencies in all three areas.) Additionally, international students were also placed in some of these courses because, while they had completed their ESL classes, many were not yet

TRISH LINDSEY JAGGERS

proficient—particularly in English composition. Many of those in our Academic Support classrooms were Arabic-speaking international students (Saudi Arabs).

My narrative prompt stems from a published essay we read in class. The author concludes her narrative with, "It was one of the hardest things I'd ever done." After a class reading of the essay, their assignment is to write a personal narrative about a difficult issue/problem they've experienced/survived, overcome/circumvented. I remind the students that they *did indeed* survive (else they would not be in that chair) and they alone control their topic this time around, *and* by controlling it *on the page*, they reduce its power to further hurt them. However, I'm often given glimpses into areas of their lives where I'm forced to make difficult decisions—from both an educator's stance and a human perspective.

Several semesters ago, one of my Saudi Arab students wrote about his mother, how close they were, how she nurtured him, catered to every detail of his life. He wrote of her eyes, her hair, her fragrance, her hands. In exquisite detail (the RENNS, "show-don't-tell," part of the assignment), he showed her caring for him through his illnesses, preparing his favorite foods, talking with him during "tough" times, and being the anchor of the ship he wished to reboard after he completed his education abroad. The "hard thing" he chose to discuss occurred in his homeland after he'd arrived in the States: His father's decision to take a second wife (a much younger one) and how his beloved mother crumpled under the news and subsequently left his father (not acceptable in his culture). An ocean away, this student's entire world was coming apart.

The feminist in me, knowing the oppression and abuses levied against Saudi women, screamed in support of his mother. I had to weigh my pedagogical "duty" against my personal distaste for that patriarchal culture. After all, I had invited him to "tell me" his personal calamity, and my role as educator must first be towards the assignment he struggled to complete and not to preach at him for the only culture he'd ever known.

During his essay revision stages, he came to my office several times per week over the next three weeks—first for composition guidance and, finally, for personal advice—and I began to notice the changes in him. Dark rings formed around his reddened eyes; his shoulders slumped; his hair was disheveled; his clothes hung loose. He was losing both sleep and weight. His voice grew so soft I could hardly hear him. His hands shook—whether from weakness or nervousness, it was hard to tell. Depression ate at him like ants. My heart ached for this young man whose culture I could not endorse (and secretly did not wish to). I realized that, in my own mind, I'd created and reached an impasse simply because I was not accepting of his culture's prescripts. I had a choice to make: Either turn away and leave

90

this student to his own devices (which were sadly inefficacious, given his pitiful physical condition at that time) or offer what I did have: My time.

I am not a counselor. However, at each office visit, I opened the floor for him to talk. He *needed* to talk about it, needed to understand it. I know part of him was needing to understand why his father would choose another wife when he had a loving one already. The other part was trying to understand why his mother would protest what both her culture and her religion dictate and approve. I told him change comes from observation, by understanding our limitations and working toward change in ourselves. Week by week, we worked through this as though it were a pile of research—*what can you change? (nothing), what can you offer? (love and support), what in your own life can you change? What will you change?* He said he would choose a life-mate—one. He would not force her to endure what his mother endured by selecting another wife. He would be the change he wished to see in his own culture. By the end of the semester, he looked rested and settled. He'd traveled home and spent time with his mother over spring break. I had not asked him to question his faith or his culture. I had not superimposed my beliefs or feminist ideologies on him; he did not need further judgment from another American. He needed understanding and guidance to help him appreciate he *already* possessed the tools necessary to survive and grow through trauma. That he trusted me, a woman in a culture alien to his own (one that often devalues its women), that he still stops by to chat and fill me in on family happenings indicates I approached this precisely the way I should have.

Again, I am not a counselor. As a reader of their personal accounts, my advice is often sought, and when asked for (or not), I am as truthful and wise as my years and experience allow. Young women who write that they are still pining for the boyfriend who left them for someone else are advised to take stock of themselves, to assess why they feel they deserve to be second best in anyone's life; to stop allowing others' opinions of them to inform and shape their opinions of themselves; to allow love into their lives and not allow shallow relationships couched as love to control their destinies; to learn to recognize those who would extort them and look for, instead, those who will exalt them. Young men are given similar advice. Students whose sexual orientations clash with the beliefs of their families come to me for shelter from their external and internal storms. Sometimes I am unprepared for the strength and force of these storms.

THE BLUE BOOK

Three years ago, as I sat reading through the week's narrative drafts, I came to a rather thick one titled "The Blue Book." (Usually, first drafts are

91

as sparse as the writer can get away with, not thick like this one.) This young writer began his essay by thoroughly describing a book, his book: A deep, rich blue with gold lettering, thin, gilded pages whose corners are bent and edges are "bunched" from being folded back and thumbed through. His book's "back is broken and scarred." (Three years later, I remember specific words he used and the power they held. I will call this student CJ for clarity though CJ is neither his name nor his initials.) This book was precious to him. In his past, he turned to it for its wisdom and guidance. In his essay, he repeatedly turns to it for answers.

After the book's description (and my, by then, essay-burned brain's befuddlement at where this paper is going), CJ recounted after-church Sunday lunches at his family's dining table, his church's pastor and a few members of the church also there as honored guests. He said the table conversation always turned to "God hates fags," and "hell's fires are being stoked for queers," and how the United States has turned into a country "encouraging of sinners" by "allowing fags to walk among us." I remember stopping there for a moment. I remembered the book he described in loving and vivid detail, his cherished book. At that moment, I *knew* where this narrative was headed.

CJ's essay continued with his pained silence at the table, his feeling certain they knew his "secret." Why else would they be discussing homosexuality so in-depth in his presence? He explained how he always knew he was different, how his sexuality never "evolved" into homosexuality, that it was there from as early as he could remember. He loved his family *and* his church—most specifically, he loved that "Blue Book." He outlined the number of times he'd turned to his book, looking for answers. "Does God hate me? If so, why did God make me?" The answers he sought were not there. Pistol-whipped by his own Bible. His essay darkened as he expressed fears of being "found out" and how he'd rather his family not have to be hurt by knowing the truth.

Here is where the story can turn. Here is where I can comment on the quality of his composition, the specificity and clarity of his details, the varied complexity of his sentences. I can praise his essay's organization, his paragraphs' transitions, his conclusion. Here is where I can return his essay for revision—revision that has no purpose other than to please a grammar guard or a rhetoric reveler. Here is where I know CJ is seeking "permission," where he has readied a reason to support a decision he is already entertaining.

So I wrote a lengthy response to his essay—first remarking on its beauty, clarity, and poignancy. Then, I gently entered this trusted space created by my student. Again, I pushed aside my inclination to fault his family's beliefs or vilify his church (incredibly difficult). I knew that to even broach those areas negatively could spell disaster. Instead, I invited him to my office so we could discuss the essay the way it deserved.

That afternoon, CJ knocked on my office door. As he took a seat, I saw the tears in his eyes. This sweet child was heartbroken. He told me he'd never told a soul about his sexuality, not even his best friend; he trusted no one to keep his secret safe from his family. He loved his family, his church, that blue book, yet he'd been taught homosexuality went against God and that homosexuals were to be loathed and avoided. Secretly, I worried that suicide, which also counters religious teachings, might also be considered. From small hints throughout our conversation, I realized I was correct in my assumptions. Neither of us had spoken the "word," but it hung in the air like a fragrance. In a flash of cognizance, I knew I once again had choices to make, and these had best be the right ones.

First, I must put a card in his hand (from our student counseling center). Next, I knew that I should not tell him that his dying would hurt his family. My reasoning was: If anyone ever needs a reason to complete suicide, revenge is as good as any. After all, how many times has he suffered through hurtful words flung around his dinner table? Is it someone else's time to suffer? My mind was burrowing for the right words, if there ever were any. I reminded CJ that his creator does not make mistakes (the Bible says so), that a child of the devil could never have a personal relationship with God, and that God made CJ exactly the way he is. Perfect. In His image. And one day, others will see beyond his sexual orientation and see this truth, too. *It will take time.* I remember saying that over and over.

I remember his relaxing, and I felt alleviated, too. I told him, "You are at college now. You are building a life for yourself, one you and only you get to live." And again, I repeated, "It will take time." We got down to the business of revising "The Blue Book," one of the most powerful essays I've been privileged to read.

In her narrative prompt, a colleague includes instructions for students not to make her cry. This is the way she protects herself, I'm sure. I do not set my narrative prompt with the intent to be made "sad," but I do not set boundaries or limit my own liability by constricting their topics. No, I am not a counselor, but I've found myself time and again in that role. There is always a student with a story that needs to be told, and their writing, when "heard," unlocks that prisoner of pain who has been begging for release. And then, I have choices to make.

CJ met with me often that semester and the semesters following, and while (the last I heard) his family still does not know, his circle of friends has widened, and he is no longer a prisoner of the closet he'd once been locked in.

TAKEAWAYS

- The author of this chapter made a conscious decision to give of her time to the students, which is also necessary when approaching a student in need. In the two scenarios shared, it is clear that the faculty member feels comfortable taking time to meet with each student and extend support and advice and to allow the student to talk about their frustrations and concerns. When working with a student in distress, try to work with both the "student" as well as the "person;" that is, maintain clear boundaries about academic expectations and be able to provide personal support while helping the students get their work done.

- Being open and building a rapport with students can help you connect to and develop a level of trust for the students to share their stories in a private space.

- It is important to recognize and consider your own biases and prescripts about cultural factors when helping the student. Be careful not to attempt to push your beliefs and values onto the student and push aside any inclination to judge based on those beliefs, background, and experiences.

- Simply listening, supporting, and, when appropriate, referring students to counseling, letting a student lean on you while maintaining clear boundaries and expectations are effective ways to engage with a student in distress. Let the student do the required work. Treat them in a sensitive manner, but not like they are fragile or weak.

- A faculty member in a situation like in this narrative would always have the option of referring the student to counseling, particularly if the student seemed to need more time and support than the faculty member can give. Agreeing to a division of labor, so to speak, is acceptable. There are some topics that faculty would prefer to not discuss with the student; those can be delegated to counseling and the faculty member can stay focused on more course-related issues. Faculty may find it easier to just recommend the student go for one visit to see what the counseling center can offer, which can be an easier message for students to hear versus being told they need counseling. It frames the situation in a way that gives the student more credit and control over their decisions.

- Get to know campus resources and have information readily available about counseling resources to give to the student. Faculty should be aware of and have campus and community resources readily available for students in distress. For example, the author

94

could have recommended the student visit the LGBTQA center on campus or attend meetings of the LGBTQA support group. Faculty who are not aware of other resources on campus could consult with fellow faculty members, the counseling center, residence hall staff, or the Dean of Students' office.

■ In this narrative, the author offered advice to one of the students. In helping someone, there may well be times you wish to offer advice in an effort to reassure them because sharing a personal experience with someone is one way to show understanding. It feels natural because with our friends and loved ones we give advice as a way to help. However, giving advice should be avoided or used sparingly as it can compromise effective helping. If you give advice, be cautious that students will not always listen, but might blame you if you give them advice that fails. If you decide to share advice, first make sure the student wants to hear it because not everyone wants advice, even if they could potentially benefit immensely from it. Instead of giving advice, it would be better to listen to the student and act as a facilitator as they find their own answers, choose solutions, and reflect on their choices and options.

■ If you are comfortable doing so, be aware of the fact that a student is religious before bringing forth the topic with the student.

■ Faculty have a lot going on and several responsibilities, which can make it challenging to notice signs that a student is in distress. Try to be aware of warning signs and symptoms—verbal indicators, nonverbal indicators, emotional signs, and behavioral cues— so that you are able to assess, identify, and approach a student as necessary in order to help a student in emotional and mental distress. For those who have a large class or teach online, such observations will be more difficult.

■ Faculty can consider including a statement about students in distress that can be included in the syllabus, which can help a student believe you may be approached if they are in mental distress. As mentioned in this narrative, a faculty member included a narrative prompt for the students indicating the intent of the assignment was not for them to be made sad, and boundaries were set, limiting the liability by constricting topics.

■ Note that the author acknowledged she is sometimes unprepared for a student's distress and emotional experience. Recognizing your limitations and areas of discomfort is a relevant part of the helping process and, to be effective, we need to feel comfortable with supporting students through the problem-solving process of an issue. In spite of good intentions, as humans we are fallible and, at times, we may need to consult or refer to better serve those we help. Consequently, there must be a reasonable level of self-awareness on the part of the faculty member who is helping a student in distress.

QUESTIONS FOR REFLECTION

1. Everyone has personal values and beliefs that they bring to every interaction with students. What role should an instructor's personal belief system play in their interactions with students in general, and especially with students who may be in distress?

2. Faculty members are often the first point of contact for students who may be experiencing mental and/or emotional challenges. As relationships form the basis of the educational process, students often confide in their instructors to an extent that makes some faculty uncomfortable. How can you balance your role as an educator and being a caring human being?

3. When international students come to the United States, they obviously bring with them certain cultural parameters that continue to influence their attitudes, behaviors, and decisions. What obligation do educators have to respect the cultural mores many students—especially international students—often feel obligated to honor while they are in this country, even when those customs put them into conflict with their personal values?

4. Faculty have an inherent responsibility to continually update their knowledge, skills, and other competencies associated with their chosen profession. One area that has received increasing emphasis when it comes to professional development involves the relational aspect that goes hand-in-hand with their instructional responsibilities. Are you aware of your limitations when it comes to dealing with the kinds of situations described in this narrative? How can you better prepare yourself to deal with the issues presented by students?

5. A course syllabus contains a great deal of information including, for the most part, course description, objectives, outcomes, grading information, policies, and institutional resources. What are your thoughts about also including a statement about students' mental well-being and distress?

Chapter Nine

Expecting the Unexpected

Supporting a Student in Crisis

Andrea Kirk-Jenkins

In graduate programs, students who are not succeeding either academically, professionally, or personally, may be placed on a Support and Remediation Plan. This provides the student with extra support from their professors, a detailed list of expectations, as well as recommendations for how they can meet those expectations. The event that I will describe focuses on a student who was placed on a Support and Remediation Plan. I was one of the faculty members involved in creating the plan and was present at the meeting with the student. In order to maintain her confidentiality, I refer to her as Harriet.

THE EVENT

The morning started off like any typical day in the office. While I was in a meeting, Harriet had called the office and spoke with a graduate assistant (GA). The GA informed the student that I was in a meeting and asked if she could take a message. The student was crying and didn't want to leave a message. Since a contact number was not provided, I emailed the student to follow up and check-in. I figured that I would see her in class later that afternoon. Harriet never returned the email, nor was she present once the class commenced later than afternoon. About an hour and a half into the class session, a ten-minute break was allotted. A student returned from her break and informed me that Harriet was upset and crying in the bathroom. Immediately, I asked my co-instructor to continue with the class lesson while I checked on Harriet. Upon entering the bathroom, I noticed that all of the stalls in the female bathroom were open except for the handicap stall at the end. I heard someone crying hysterically and having a difficult time catching her breath. I said "Harriet. It's Dr. Jenkins." Upon which, the door to the stall quickly swung open. I walked down and saw Harriet huddled on the bathroom floor, sobbing, shaking uncontrollably, and flushed in the face.

There was another student sitting next to Harriet attempting to calm her down. I immediately crouched down and told Harriet that I was there and put my hand on her shoulder. I asked her to listen to my voice and if she would be willing to take some deep breaths with me. When she shook her head in agreement, I guided her and her classmate through some deep breathing exercises. I had them take in deep breaths through their nose, hold it and, on my count, breathe out through their mouths. We repeated this approximately five times. After this exercise, Harriet was visibly calmer. I asked her if I could help her off the bathroom floor, to which she shook her head yes.

Once Harriet was off the bathroom floor, I dismissed her classmate back to class. I asked Harriet if she felt comfortable leaving the bathroom to go sit in one of the building's common areas. These areas are typically quiet and have comfortable couches available. She agreed. Harriet began trembling a bit more and her sobbing was increasing in intensity. I led her to the couch with my arm braced around her arm and helped her sit down. I spent a few minutes speaking with her. Harriet began to share more of the symptoms she was experiencing, as well as the events occurring over the past two days that led to her current condition. Harriet also mentioned that she met with her therapist that morning and that her therapist thought it was a good idea for her to attend class this evening, as it could be a good distraction. The student then stated that she was feeling hopeless. Upon which I assessed for suicidal ideation; no indicators were present.

At this point, while she wasn't a danger to herself in the terms of suicide, I did deem that it was unsafe for her to drive the 90-minute ride home by herself. I informed her of my concern, trying to remain open and transparent with her throughout this process. She agreed that it wasn't safe to drive. Her boyfriend, whom she lives with, was currently out of the state traveling for work. She stated she had a cousin who lives in the area. We tried to call her but there was no answer. I advised the student to leave a message in hopes that she would call back.

During the initial conversation, Harriet said that she didn't have any other family or friends in the area or anyone she felt comfortable going to for help. I asked her if she would be willing to go to the hospital, to which she replied, no. Since there did not seem anyone available to take Harriet back home, I decided to focus more on her condition. Harriet was still shaking uncontrollably, more so than being simply upset. I asked her what she had eaten today and if she had taken her medications as prescribed. She replied that she hadn't eaten anything all day (it was 7 pm). She also admitted that she hadn't taken her medication for the past two days (i.e., both anti-anxiety/depression and thyroid medication). I asked her if she had brought any snacks; she had not. I offered her some of my snacks, as well as some of the food that I did not finish from my lunch that afternoon. She agreed to give a few things a try.

Before I went to retrieve the snacks, I focused on more ways to ground her. Knowing that her mom has been a strong support person for her, I asked Harriet how she felt about calling her mom so she could hear her voice (her mother lived a few hundred miles away). She was open to us calling her mom together and spoke with her for a few minutes. Unfortunately, the phone connection with her mother seemed to get her more upset. Her mother had a difficult time understanding her as Harriet was unable to articulate her words amidst her sobbing. Harriet handed the phone over to me and I explained to her mom that she was clearly having a bit of a rough night, attempted but was unable to attend class but was currently safe at this moment. I also expressed my concern for her and that I didn't feel it was safe for her to be driving home, to which the mother agreed. I asked her mom if she knew of anyone who could look after Harriet and possibly give her a ride home; her mom wasn't aware of anyone.

I handed the phone back to Harriet to continue to talk to her mom. Once I heard Harriet begin to discuss the events that transpired over the last two days which caused her to get upset, I whispered to her that I was going to go to my office to get some food for her to try to eat. She agreed to stay in the same location until I got back. This allowed me the opportunity to gather my thoughts and get my game plan together. While heading to my office, I was fortunate enough to see a colleague in her office and was able to consult with her about the situation. She provided me with the phone number for campus police, who is our after-hours contact for the university counseling center. The university counseling center always has someone on call who can assist in assessing a student and advising a professor on the recommended next steps. Although I knew the student wasn't suicidal, I didn't have a plan or the resources on how to get the student home safely. Incidentally, I also knew the student was a client of the counseling center (Harriet informed me).

With snacks in hand, I went back to the student, not wanting to leave her waiting for long. I felt relieved to see she was still in the same spot, on the phone with her mom. I handed her some snacks (granola bar, an orange, and peanut butter crackers) and asked her to try at least one of them. In order to maintain transparency, I explained to her that I was going to call the counseling office to speak to the on-call therapist. She seemed relieved with that information and said she was going to continue to speak with her mom. I went back to my office and dialed campus police who transferred me to the on-call therapist.

When speaking with the on-call therapist, I reviewed the student's symptoms as well as my own observations. While the student believed she was having a panic attack, we both believed that her symptoms (sobbing, dysregulated breathing) were lasting far longer than one would expect for those of a panic attack. I joked with the therapist that we just covered a related topic in class an hour ago, so it was luckily still fresh in my mind. We discussed her thyroid issues and the fact that she hadn't taken her medication as prescribed and thought it could be a combination of both physical and emotional concerns. The on-call therapist's recommendation was for her to go to the emergency room to be examined. I noted my concern about Harriet's hesitancy. He said to give her three different options 1) she can get a ride to the emergency room, 2) we can call campus police to take her or 3) she can wait it out until she feels safe to drive home if she couldn't find a ride. I thanked him for his recommendations and returned back to my student.

Harriet had eaten the orange and part of the granola bar. I shared what the on-call therapist and I discussed; that she was possibly struggling with something medical as well as emotional. I provided psychoeducation, explaining the symptoms and typical duration of a panic attack while comparing them to her current symptoms. Additionally, with gentleness as well as assertiveness, I explained to her that we thought the best option was for her to go to the hospital. While reluctant at first, mostly due to the cost, she agreed to go to get assessed. When I asked if there was anyone she was comfortable asking to take her (since it was closer than driving her home), she named four students from the class. One of the students she mentioned was the student who was in the bathroom stall with her. Believing that this student was a good resource, I concurred that she may be a good option. I went into class, which was wrapping up shortly, and asked the student if she would be willing to take Harriet to the emergency room. She was happy to do so.

I returned to Harriet and informed her that her classmate would be taking her to the hospital. Harriet seemed relieved. I continued to do more grounding techniques (deep breathing and guided imagery) with Harriet. We also discussed the importance of self-care since she repeatedly said how disappointed she was in herself. I reminded her that self-care is similar to riding on an airplane. We always need to put on our oxygen mask first before assisting others, in the event of an emergency. I needed her to put on her oxygen mask and take care of herself before she thought of and returned to her counseling courses.

Once the student who was taking Harriet to the hospital came out of class, the three of us discussed the different hospital options and back-up plans. I asked the student peer to remain in contact with me regarding Harriet's status. Harriet thanked me profusely for being there for her and headed out with her friend. Once the student left, I briefed my co-instructor on the events of the evening and thanked her for covering my class. I then text messaged my department head and our clinical coordinator to inform them of the events that transpired that evening. Much later that evening, Harriet's friend informed me that the results of Harriet's bloodwork indicated that her thyroid levels were off. However, she was able to drive home on her own and stayed on the phone with someone during her drive. We eventually received confirmation that she made it home safely that evening.

The next morning, Harriet emailed me, thanking me again and informing me more in depth of her test results. Her medication was adjusted by her doctors and she was informed that it should take two weeks before the full effects would be felt. She mentioned that she was still experiencing similar feelings and thoughts as she did the night previously. I recommended that she not return back to campus to attend another class that evening. I followed-up again with my department head. She agreed that Harriet should not attend class that evening but should focus on practicing self-care. We scheduled a follow-up support phone meeting with Harriet for the following morning.

During the support meeting, the department head and I made a recommendation for the student to take a medical leave of absence so that she could focus on stabilizing her medical issues, as well as addressing her mental and emotional health. Harriet declined this recommendation, stating that she would be on the mend. The department head and I agreed to compromise with Harriet. However, we noted that the compromise would last only if Harriet could address her medical and mental health concerns in such ways that did not impede her success in the program. The following week, Harriet was 45 minutes late for both of her classes. As a result, Harriet was placed on a Level 2 Support and Remediation plan that included revisions and caution that the next result in the support and remediation plan could be termination from the program.

AN EVENT AMONGST MANY

This student had been on a support plan for over a year due to medical and mental health issues which were impacting her academic performance. There had been previous cases with other professors of the student arriving late for class, not showing, or needing to leave early; however, this was the first time the student appeared to be in a state of crisis. On one occasion the student had a seizure the day before and felt faint towards the end of class. She told the professor who came up to check on her and they were able to arrange an Uber to take her home. Another time when the student's health was declining, her mom was staying with her for the month and taking her to and from classes. On one occasion, Harriet's mother waited for her in the hallway during an eight-hour Saturday lecture. While this student is someone who was provided with extra support since learning about her challenges, we have increased our support offered to the student and have been continuously checking in since the event during class.

SUPPORT OF THE PROFESSOR

Fortunately, during the crisis as well as afterwards, I felt supported by my colleagues. During the actual event, another professor was in the office who was extremely familiar with university policy and procedure. I consulted with her regarding appropriate protocol and was able to process the event. She provided me with the contact number for the campus police, which is the university policy for reaching the on-call counselor. Thankfully, I also had the support of our adjunct instructor who was able to cover class so the other 30 students were not impacted by the crisis. Once the student had left for the evening, I informed my department head as well as my other colleagues who work with this student about what had occurred. I found them to be supportive, helpful, and validating.

PREPAREDNESS

Expect the unexpected seems to work well in teaching. Fortunately, my whole educational career as well as clinical experience had prepared me for that experience. Due to my crisis training, I was able to remain calm, think clearly, and be non-reactionary. I knew that I had the capabilities and skill set to calm the student down and assess her for safety. I was also cognizant during this event that, while I am a counselor, I was not Harriet's counselor. My role was to help calm her in such a way that she could and would be open to assistance from others. I still had a class of 30 students waiting for me. The biggest curve ball was learning the university protocol, responsibility, as well as my own liability as a professor while the event was transpiring. Again, it was the community of support that helped me move through this process successfully.

TAKEAWAYS

- As described in this narrative, the author had to leave her class of 30 students in order to help the distressed student regulate her symptoms. In this case, there was a co-instructor; however, if she did not have a co-instructor, she would have still been obligated to help the student and would have had to consider how to manage her class. It is likely that the class would have had to be cancelled in order to maintain priority focus on the distressed student. The important lesson here is this—don't attempt to manage both simultaneously.

- Some potential strategies to use when helping a student in distress are breathing techniques, consultation, assessment of the student's suicidal ideation, and follow up with the student.

- As mentioned in the narrative, put your own oxygen mask on before you help others put theirs on. Take a deep breath. We can sometimes be so drawn into a crisis that we do not take the moments we need to center and ground ourselves. However, be sure to ground yourself and intentionally relax. Take two minutes to do it.

- Observe the student's behavior and assess if the student is safe. Share your observations, including relevant background, and get a second opinion from the professional. Be sure to also document your actions in helping the student.

- Know university policies and procedures as well as resources available to assist a student in distress. It is advisable that departments share such information with faculty (i.e., related to support offices and recommendations about what to do when a student is in distress).

- Consider that it is likely that a student is not only struggling with a mental and emotional condition, but also with a physical and medical one. If your attempts to help a student calm themselves are not working, there may be a medical condition interfering with the student's ability to regulate. Again, this is why it is actually important to refrain from assumptions and diagnoses. Remember, only trained professionals should ever make formal diagnoses. In such cases, asking that the student visit the emergency room for a formal medical assessment at the hospital is imperative. If a student needs to receive medical attention, be genuine and clear in explaining the next steps to the student.

- Follow up is a crucial part of the helping process as it demonstrates genuine care and also communicates that you are another resource for a student. The department in this narrative had a process in place for student support, review, and remediation, which provided the author with an avenue to discuss how to best serve the distressed student. The support team identifies and supports students who exhibit academic or behavioral problems by providing early systematic assistance, remediation plans, and, if needed, a plan to connect them to appropriate interventions and support. If your department does not have such a support system in place, consider developing one. If having such a team is not of interest, be sure to keep all stakeholders in the loop about the distressed student.

103

■ Discussing a plan for self-care with the student (see Chapter 8 of Burke, Sauerheber, Hughey, & Laves, 2017 for a self-care and wellness plan worksheet) is also a worthwhile option when helping a student in distress.

QUESTIONS FOR REFLECTION

1. As illustrated in this narrative, faculty and staff are often caught off-guard by some episodes, such as the one described. Although sometimes there are clues that something is not quite right with a student, it can still be potentially overwhelming when dramatic and potentially dangerous events start to unfold. How comfortable would you be having to leave the other students in your class to respond to the immediate needs of a student in distress? What types of support would you expect if you encountered a student like the one described in this narrative?

2. Everyone who works on a college campus needs to have a basic understanding of how these situations can arise and what should be done in the moment to deal with their potentially devastating consequences—both in the short term as well as the long term. What knowledge, skills, and competencies do you believe every person who works on a college campus should have in order to be prepared to successfully intervene when these situations occur?

3. Faculty and staff are often required to balance the needs of the institution with the needs of the individual student. Reflect on your own philosophy of higher education and determine whether you lean more toward meeting the needs of an individual student or protecting the integrity of the educational process. Where do you fall on this continuum? Is your perspective compatible with your personal values and beliefs? Is it compatible with your obligations to your department and/or profession?

4. As noted, self-care is very important. Faculty members also have mental/emotional needs and situations like these can be very draining. Do you feel that you give the appropriate attention to maintaining your own physical, mental, and emotional well-being? How do you take better care of yourself?

REFERENCE

Burke, M. G., Sauerheber, J. D., Hughey, A. W., & Laves, K. (2017). *Helping skills for working with college students: Applying counseling theory to student affairs practice.* New York, NY: Routledge.

Chapter Ten

Hidden Triggers Revealing Students in Abusive Relationships

Theresia Johnson-Ratliff

Field education in a graduate program is one of the most rewarding and challenging experiences of a graduate student. Students are eager to apply classroom knowledge, skills, and values to real-life practice experiences. As a director of field education in a graduate program, I am excited to coach students through this transitional period. I look forward to witnessing the amazement on a student's face when he or she completes a psychosocial assessment or is a part of an interdisciplinary treatment team. The many years of experience in field education allows me to also witness when past experiences of students are triggered in the pre-field placement interview. Students suddenly realize "this is real" and many are confronted with critical situations that are like their past experiences. Furthermore, I concede that these triggers of critical past experiences apply to both traditional and nontraditional students. This narrative identifies triggers that lead a traditional and non-traditional student to emotional and physical outbursts during a pre-field placement interview in a graduate program on a satellite campus. The narrative also demonstrates strategies used to work with the distressed student.

Students enter our graduate program from a variety of communities throughout the United States and, consequently, they have diverse cultural beliefs and norms. They also come with different attitudes and perspectives of a graduate program as well as ideas and perspectives of a graduate student. We have students who honestly search for the truth through knowledge. Some students come with an attitude of self-righteousness in the form of knowing everything they need to know about a graduate program. Soon, these students learn their self-righteousness is just that, "self," and only serves them, especially as they encounter bruises and bumps along the way that take a long time to heal. Students who are culturally encapsulated and supercilious often require spoon feeding, which is challenging for professors.

In addition, there are those students who think they have all the answers, but quickly realize they have planted their seeds of concepts on thorny soil, and cannot expand their personal or professional growth, development or knowledge, because of their own misguided concepts and choices. These students have developed and accepted their bad habits and come into the program expecting faculty, staff, other students, and everyone else to tolerate their bad habits as well. Although these students will present themselves as having it together, eventually those concepts planted on thorny soil will appear and the student has difficulty in conceptualizing right from wrong.

Finally, I have engaged students who planted their seeds of concepts on solid ground but did not have the confidence to follow through and, therefore, went back to pick up their seeds. In picking up the seeds, the students found the seeds were rotten, but kept the seeds and, as a result, brought rotten seeds (i.e., baggage) with them to the graduate program to spread and persuade others to "follow" them. This type of student also attempts to influence faculty and staff by sharing the baggage to gain sympathy and additional support.

This narrative focuses on the traditional student who plants her seed on thorny ground and the non-traditional student who plants her seeds on solid ground but goes back to pick up rotten seeds. However, in each scenario, the student felt comfortable enough to share their trauma with me and I felt comfortable enough to allow them their moments.

As Director of Field Education for a graduate program, I am responsible for engaging in pre-field placement interviews, which is for students entering their first field placement and occurs approximately between 3 to 12 months after their initial orientation. Only meeting for a second time since the orientation, the student and I meet privately in my office, which is located on a small satellite campus where there is little foot traffic. The pre-field placement interview consists of reviewing demographic information from the pre-field placement application submitted by the student and academic questions related to courses they have completed.

THE TRADITIONAL GRADUATE STUDENT

This student was around 23 years of age and had lived in the Northeastern region of the United States prior to attending our graduate program. During orientation the student was very poised, self-assured, appropriately dressed, and demonstrated critical thinking skills. The student was active in the graduate program and expected other students, faculty, and staff to cater to her. Although she was active, she was not always punctual in completing assignments and tasks and did not view this behavior as a problem.

She arrived at the appointment early and, upon entering my office, she exhibited her usual traits—poised, self-assured, and appropriately dressed, with a pen and tablet.

A section of the interview focuses on skills from a practice class. The student was asked to define empathy and to participate in a role-play applying the definition of empathy while engaging with a client. Of course, this question is an important component of inquiry as empathy is critical in the helping professions because it allows the student to understand clients' diverse emotions, direct their focus appropriately, and communicate an understanding of the client's emotions while applying limited self-disclosure. The student successfully defined empathy as "the ability to understand another person's emotions while putting yourself in that person's shoes." I then directed the student to engage in a role-play with me, responding to the client with no more than three empathetic sentences relying on the definition of empathy.

The student and I engaged in the role-play with the student identifying as the social worker and I as the client. The role-play scenario is as follows:

> A 13-year-old Black female has been in foster care since the age of three months. She has been in several foster care homes. She comes to the social worker's office and says she has a secret. The secret is she is fearful and scared to take a bath because she might drown.

After several attempts, the student was unable to respond with three empathetic sentences to the client's emotions. I decided to assist the student through coaching which is a critical part of the learning process for students. Coaching helps students to think critically and apply classroom knowledge to practice through a series of leading sentences and buzzwords. Coaching with this student involved reviewing the definition of empathy and applying each segment of empathy to the role-play. After several interventions with the client (me), the social worker (student) is unable to respond effectively (apply empathetic responses) to the role-play situation.

I then demonstrated correct and applicable empathetic responses to the student. She was receptive and agreed she should have been able to respond with empathy appropriately. I begin to tell her how empathy helps to build rapport with clients and leads to a trusting client/worker relationship. I shared with her an incident that occurred when I was in the beginning stage of my helping professional career and a woman came into the emergency room where I worked who had been severely beaten and choked by her boyfriend. After providing details, I then proceeded to tell her that the woman said she was embarrassed because she felt people stared at her and whispered about her. I was about to tell the student how I applied empathy to the woman; however, the student immediately began to cry uncontrollably, and walked around the office shaking her head and flinging her arms. I gave her a tissue and watched her for several minutes and asked her if she wanted water, which I also keep inside my desk drawer. She accepted the tissue, but not the water.

After approximately five minutes of crying and pacing, the student apologized. She explained that she came to the university from another state to escape an abusive relationship with her boyfriend. She said her abuser choked her several times. After reporting him to the authorities, he then began harassing her by sitting in his car outside her home and showing up where she worked or shopped. I asked her if my sharing of the incident of the woman coming to the emergency room made her think about her abusive boyfriend. She replied that she began thinking about her incident when I said the child had a *secret* in the role-play. The student admitted this secret was embarrassing and hindered her from moving forth in her academic, professional, and personal development. Although she participated in numerous activities, the secret held her back, which caused her at times to exhibit anger and privileged behavior.

I thanked her for sharing her feelings and situation. I then reassured her that I wanted to see her succeed in the program and referred her to the two student counseling centers on the main campus. I also reminded her that my role is to assist her with professional and academic advisement.

This experience with the student left me bewildered in the sense that I initially thought the student's behavior was a result of engaging in the role-play. I was surprised to learn that it was only one word from the role-play that triggered the student's emotional outburst. A valuable lesson that I learned is to be aware of invisible triggering words that might lead to a student's emotional outburst. Another lesson for me is not to downplay the significance of a student's emotional state in spite of the fact that they appear to have it together and move successfully through in matriculation.

I followed up with this student through several phone calls. She also periodically stopped by my office to say hello and reported that she was doing well. This student graduated from the program and went on to become a successful professional in another state.

THE NONTRADITIONAL STUDENT

The nontraditional student was late for her appointment. She explained that she had to "take care of some things, which made her late," but offered no words of apology to me. I also remembered that this student was late for the program's orientation. However, she participated in orientation by asking appropriate questions and engaging with other students. The student, who is approximately 45 years of age, was poised, well dressed, and appeared eager to move forth with the interview. Before engaging in the pre-field placement interview process, she began to talk about her past life experiences and her decision to obtain a graduate degree in a helping profession.

The student explained that she perceives herself as highly intelligent but made some bad choices in life. She shared that she was a top student in high school and in the undergraduate program. She married very young and did not pursue higher education because her husband was a minister. She went on to explain that she loved her husband and two children, and she went beyond expectations to support her husband in the ministry. However, she was married for 17 years to an emotionally abusive husband and she recently got the courage to divorce him. The student described the emotional abuse as in the form of yelling, cursing, putting her down in public, as well as often calling her dumb and stupid. She expounded that because of her life's experiences, she could help students in this program and, after graduating, could help other women facing similar marriage challenges.

The nontraditional student described in detail the humiliation it caused her to divorce her husband, who is now seen in public with another woman. The divorce was finalized two months before her husband publicly dated another woman. I noticed the student was sweating and began to silently weep. I offered her a tissue and water and she accepted both. As she composed herself, she began to explain that she wanted the faculty to know about the abuse she experienced and how it impacted her decision to further her education in a helping profession. She shared her bitterness towards her husband and her desire to educate women married to ministers about not accepting emotional abuse simply due to their spouse's profession in the ministry and the veneration from others that often accompanies this position.

This student shared that she was in counseling and it was helping her to accept that she made the right choice to divorce her husband. She admitted to feeling guilty about the divorce and not pleasing God. I tried several times to steer the conversation to the pre-field placement interview process; however, the student ignored my attempts to redirect and continued to repeatedly discuss her feelings of anger, guilt, and humiliation associated with the divorce of a minister.

In my experience, I have noticed that nontraditional students enjoy sharing their life experiences with others, which is acceptable at the correct time. I finally relinquished the idea of the pre-field placement interview and recommended that she reschedule when she was ready to proceed. She agreed that it was best to reschedule the interview. The student admitted she continues to "pick up" and give credence to the words and past actions of her husband and how her picking it up keeps her from reaching her goals. I recommended she talk with her therapist about a support group for divorcees.

The triggering factor for this student was the opportunity to work with women who experienced emotional abuse from their husbands. She wanted to be sure that I understood that trigger before she entered the interview process. I believe that I needed to allow this student the opportunity to ventilate her feelings before successfully moving forth with her pre-field placement interview. In the past, I was a stickler for maintaining a scheduled process. Setting boundaries is important, but listening is more important in student–faculty relationships.

TAKEAWAYS

- Sometimes, faculty's topic of discussion in the classroom or meetings can prompt unpleasant memories and feelings for students. For those who teach courses that include topics that are sensitive in nature, it could be beneficial to think about how you will respond to a student who reports being in distress because of the course topic. Moreover, research suggests that one's religious/spiritual beliefs and the role they play in one's life can be substantial considerations in the coping process.
- There are times when we cannot just focus on the process (e.g., advising, interviewing) in our meetings with students. We must be intuitive about those moments when we just need to take time to engage with the student and pause the process. Allow the student time to cry and decompress in silence. It would be beneficial if faculty have tissues in their offices to offer in moments of student distress.
- Following up with students, whether in passing or via email, can play a role in the student's coping process as they feel there is someone who cares. Even if a student presents themselves as "having it all together" this does not detract from the fact there could be traumatic events and pressures in their lives that could contribute to their distress.
- You can never know what is going on in a student's life at any given moment. Therefore, it is important to be sensitive to the reactions you may encounter when engaging with students, such

as those described in this narrative. Emotional reactions can be triggered by a number of events and faculty must be prepared to respond to these adverse reactions in a manner that meets their individual needs while preserving the integrity of the process for everyone involved.

- Having empathy is essential to facilitating the helping process and it is a critical ingredient when attempting to deal with students in distress. Some students seem to be naturally empathetic, while others struggle when trying to connect with others on a deeper level. Faculty and staff need to realize that students have widely varying capacities for demonstrating empathy and adjust their approach when attempting to respond to their needs accordingly.

- Many of today's students bring a tremendous amount of emotional baggage with them to the college campus. Many factors have contributed to this reality, especially since access to higher education is much more universal and egalitarian than in the past. The prevalence of mental and emotional conditions and diagnoses among the student population has increased substantially; as such, faculty and staff must adjust their approach to dealing with students accordingly.

- Age has to be taken into consideration when responding to students who are experiencing distress. Older students who are attending college bring with them a diverse set of formative experiences and cultural reference points that may be completely outside the comprehension of many of their younger peers (and even of many faculty, staff, and administrators). Older students also exhibit anxiety and stress in a way that is often qualitatively different than their younger peers.

- Including information in a course syllabus or field experience manual that informs students of possible course content or activities that might stir up unresolved issues can be helpful. Students benefit from knowing that strong emotional reactions are possible and quite normal and that students are welcome to excuse themselves if necessary as well as using campus services (e.g., counseling center, women's center) for additional assistance.

- Many of us struggle with telling a student that we are not the one to provide help, especially if we think that we will appear as selfish or unsupportive. Practice how you would say the words before the situation occurs and make it a natural expression that sets boundaries but also provides a helpful referral.

QUESTIONS FOR REFLECTION

1. When you are talking to a student, how often do you think about if you are using "triggering" words?
2. If presenting a topic in the classroom that could possibly trigger an unpleasant emotion for a student, do you prepare for such an outcome? If so, how? If not, why not?
3. What are your thoughts on remaining in a student's support circle while they are matriculating through your academic program? What do you think about remaining a part of a student's support system beyond graduation?
4. If a student brings forth a topic of conversation that is unpleasant and does not want to move on from that topic, but you do, would you redirect the conversation? If so, how would you do so? If not, why would you choose to let them continue?
5. What is your comfort level with discussing religion and spirituality as a coping mechanism for a student?
6. Age differences in the classroom are becoming the norm rather than the exception. When students are distressed, what are some qualitative differences in the ways the different generations manifest anxiety?
7. Many of today's college students have complicated lives. How much should outside responsibilities be taken into account when dealing with a student in distress?
8. Obviously, a student's family life, parental obligations, health considerations, and employment situation contribute to their overall anxiety and stress levels. When a student does act in a manner that is counterproductive to the educational process, should these outside influences be considered as mitigating factors?

Chapter Eleven

When a Student's Bad Relationship Got Worse

Leigh Johnson-Migalski

During my office hours close to the term break, Michelle (a pseudonym), a current student of mine, stopped by. Michelle was a well-known student on campus and was active in leadership positions on and off campus. I had her in graduate courses prior to this, but her academic performance was different this time. During the term, she had been a little inconsistent with attendance and, although her work was not as high quality as in the past, she was doing just good enough in the course. I simply thought she was having young adult problems that are common to many of us during that phase of our lives.

My door was propped open as Michelle stood in the doorway requesting to chat. Dejected, she sat in the chair as I quickly closed the door. For part of our discussion she hid her face with her hair and, after being with her for an hour, she eventually took off her coat and backpack. During our conversation she appeared withdrawn, ambivalent about being there, and tearful. For the next three hours we talked. Her distractedness and tears made it difficult and I had to use all of the helping and communication skills in my repertoire.

Michelle explained how she was afraid of being kicked out of school because she was sent to the disciplinary committee (not the real committee's name) for having an inappropriate interaction with a co-worker in another university department where she held part-time employment. The meeting with the disciplinary committee resulted in her having to engage in Title IX processes due to the sexual assault and abuse the student experienced at the site.

Michelle had shared the experience with her family the previous weekend. She felt extreme shame because her mother, in particular, blamed her for this incident. She was confused and ambivalent because the co-worker (this person's gender identity will be concealed with they/them/their) was pursuing her through continued messaging and emails. Michelle whispered that she was exhausted from all of the Title IX procedures, the multiple meetings, her other co-workers and peers talking about her, and her poor functioning at school.

After multiple questions about the scenario, I asked Michelle how I could help her, and she responded that she was not sure as she continued to cry. I asked if she had thoughts of killing herself, to which she replied that she had but was not in treatment. She conveyed that she did not want to call the 24-hour crisis/counseling services on campus where students can get five sessions for free. She also reported feeling ambivalent about living, which made me consider her as at risk. However, she did not have a history of suicidal attempts or any family members who attempted suicide and did not have access to a weapon.

I asked Michelle why, out of all of the professors who were around, she would share her story and suicidal status with me. She replied that she did not know. I responded that I thought she knew I would help and that is why she came to me. I told her that, deep down, she knew I would understand and assist her. I also told her that although she felt that she did not know what to do, there is a part of her that does, which likely motivated her to consult with me. I also told her that because of our previous interactions she knew we could figure it out. I believe that my previous relationship with this student helped me in this situation.

I interpreted her suicidal ideation as partly related to her wanting to stop the pain that she was experiencing. She believed that she let her family down and herself down. She had survived much of her difficult life by overcompensating to be a successful student and now she felt as if she was failing. She saw herself as inadequate in the domains of family, school, and in intimate relationships. Michelle agreed about my guesses but also added that the person at the site keeps messaging her about wanting more sex and that she is thinking about meeting with them because they said they would stop messaging her if she would have sex again.

I provided psychoeducation to Michelle, detailing that interactions with this person who violated her can be confusing, especially because it was her first experience. I shared with her that it was unlikely that this person would stop, and this behavior could be viewed as not being respectful and as abusive. I spoke about how she has not had romantic experiences and, of course, she just does not have a lot of practice with this stuff. I told her many women get treated this way by society unfortunately, and that she is not alone. Even people with more romantic experience are not respected in this way. Considering our discussion thus far, I interpreted that it makes sense that she would consider suicidal ideation because it provides a solution. Part of the suicidal ideation provided relief for her because, if she was not around, then she could stop the harassing messages while also not having sex with the person again and feeling worse about herself.

I asked Michelle if she needed to go to the hospital as she continued to be ambivalent about her suicidal ideation. I told her that she could not leave my office until she called the 24-hour crisis line to set up an appointment or at least to see what her options were. She used my office phone and I told her that she did not need to put it on speaker phone. She was honest with the intake worker about her level of distress and that I was sitting with her. I think my decision in that moment to not put it on speaker phone was about not wanting the call, metaphorically, to feel like the whole word was listening; but also, I think I wanted to show that I trusted her. She was able to get an appointment within 36 hours and she guaranteed her safety.

Next, we discussed the choice that she had to not answer the messages of the individual who was pursuing her. She indicated that she may block their calls. I shared resources with her if she wanted to fill out an order of protection. Although I am not sure, I do not think she filled out a police report on this person because she knew they were already in trouble at work and they were blaming her for that trouble. I knew Michelle had more appointments with her advisor, her immediate supervisor, and the Title IX coordinator later that week. I probably should have told her advisor, but I was afraid they would immediately hospitalize her (I did not think this would be the best way of operating given our conversation). Perhaps my confidence in how we processed the situation, as well as my lack of trust of some of my colleagues, prevented me from reaching out. I was concerned about the further pathologizing of this student versus seeing the student in context; as a non-majority student who has been so successful given other tragedies in her life.

Michelle continued to check in with me by email about other topics, such as feedback from my class, over the next couple of days, but she never mentioned our meeting. Later in the next week, I received an email from the chair of the department instructing anyone to come to them if this student comes to more faculty being in distress. I now check in more with my colleagues about their students when they report being in distress. The break for the term occurred and I saw Michelle about two months later. She looked better. I told her that we needed to talk in my office while emphasizing to her that our previous chat did not change how I view her and reminding her of how successful she is in life. I told her that I would not treat her differently because I was aware of her issues and she does not need to avoid me. I was worried she would associate me with only this experience and that she would feel shame since I knew what happened. Addressing how our relationship could be in the

115

future helped our interactions continue. I celebrated with her over the next couple of years with her success with various conference poster presentations, the defense of her master's thesis, and her placement at highly competitive training sites.

My reflections on this experience range. First, when I first started teaching years ago, I tried to lead as a "stand-offish to be feared" authority to stave off the challenges from students that often happen to professors of my presenting gender. I soon found that I flourish when I am authentic in my class governance with my socio-cultural identities and operate in a kind but firm manner. I lead with love and encouragement versus fear while maintaining appropriate boundaries. I focus on building relationships with my students so that there is foundation to construct future mentoring or that, when challenged, I have credibility in focus on students' growth areas. I trust that Michelle likely came to me because of how I present myself to my students. On the other hand, at the time of this conversation, I felt sad and livid at the sexual incident and the continued abuse/stalking by the non-clinical staff member.

I felt angry at the processes that the student was going through, particularly the remediation plan. However, I only heard her side and have no idea what other probable avoidance behaviors she may have engaged in just to survive the past couple of months. I was also nervous about her suicidal ideation and making sure that she was going to be safe. I knew I could handle it, but I was also wondering how I was going to get her there. Call 911? Call campus security? There was also another element to this situation. Additionally, I also felt annoyed when this student came to my office. I knew she needed me, but I also desired those three hours to complete grading and other tasks. The annoyance that I experienced was likely more related to feeling burnt out at the end of the term and trying to juggle parental duties. In short, I am grateful to God that I was there for that student and that I could be used by Him in this way. I think about how this student is flourishing now and how she can help so many people in the future.

I believe faculty will continue to assist suicidal students in the future. More of our students will have backgrounds and foregrounds of people who will have been targeted by violence and trauma given to them, especially considering the rise of violence toward Black people. The violence and trauma are in our classrooms now. It trickles down too into our offices. We can be turning points for our students. We can be the change agent to help them, and possibly others, through our work, although we need support and resources to do that. What would I have done without the 24-hour crisis line? What if I did not have the necessary knowledge from my pre-academic life? As more faculty are given contracts instead of tenure, more faculty are asked to produce and publish, and to be cognizant of financial limitations, can we help our students the way we need to? How do we get the needed specific training, particularly the faculty who are not in the fields of social work, counseling, or psychology?

TAKEAWAYS

- Initially, the student did not convey (verbally or nonverbally) that she was having suicide ideation. It is so important to listen carefully and ask the question, "are you thinking about hurting yourself?"
- It is not uncommon for a partner dealing with another partner's aggressive advances to want to "disappear." Sometimes this feels more doable than actually facing the partner and putting up boundaries. It is very important to understand how difficult it can be to break the ties from an aggressive pursuer (the dynamics can have an addictive nature).
- This situation illustrates the importance of being open and upfront with students and letting them know as soon as possible your obligations when discussing certain topics like sexual harassment, sexual assault, or suicidal thoughts, without discouraging them from talking. Having a statement in your syllabus can let students know from day one that they are welcome to talk with you and that you will act in their best interests, and possibly involve others, if certain topics come up in the conversation.
- Suicide is a difficult topic; it often stirs up a lot of anxiety for faculty members when they find out a student is thinking about suicide. Additional training can be helpful and many universities offer small group training in responding to a student that may be suicidal. Contact your Dean of Students or your Counseling Center to learn more.
- Consulting with other faculty in the department to ascertain their observations of a specific student's behavior can be beneficial, especially if the behavior merits further attention.

QUESTIONS FOR REFLECTION

1. What might get in the way of you setting aside the time that a student in crisis may need?
2. Would you feel obligated to make a report if you knew someone on campus was sexually harassing one of your students? What if the student pleaded with you not to make the report?

3. Title IX regulations can be confusing. Are you aware of what you are legally required to do when a student shares with you details of a sexual assault or harassment?
4. If a student mentions that they might hurt themselves or are suicidal, what specific steps or follow up questions will you ask?
5. If you were in this faculty's position, what steps would you have taken to address the student's distress?

Chapter Twelve

When a Student Experiences a Series of Unfortunate Events

Megan X. Schutte

In the spring semester of 2018, I took an elective titled "Gender and Sexuality in Higher Education" for my PhD program in Higher Education Administration. This class presented contemporary thinking regarding gender identity and expression (Ryle, 2018) and the traditional notions of the workplace as a gendered sphere (Acker, 1990). It also challenged us to confront our own biases surrounding these issues and confront them in an educational setting. While I actually think about sexuality and gender a lot in my everyday professional life, my *personal* identities in that realm are something I have rarely thought about because they were never in question for me. I always felt like a girl (even if a tomboyish one) and have always been attracted to men; so, my personal identities as female, feminine, and heterosexual were never something I questioned (internally). Besides, since I am cisgendered and straight, I am in the privileged position where society does not question my identity (externally) either. My understanding of gender and sexuality for others, however, has been anything but constant; on the contrary, in the past 20 or so years, I (like many people) have greatly evolved in my thinking about these issues from being a binary to existing on a spectrum.

The aforementioned class prompted me to consider these issues not just for myself, but for my students as well. As a result, I started to more deliberately and systematically work on issues of inclusion—including gender identity—in the classroom by taking the following steps: using gender-neutral terminology; using preferred names and correct pronunciation of them; and asking for and giving pronouns. I felt confident in these choices knowing that, at some point, they would be helpful to vulnerable and/or marginalized students. I just had no idea it would happen so immediately.

The next semester, I employed my new techniques in the classes I was teaching. This included having students fill out index cards with general information including preferred names, phonetic pronunciations, and pronouns on the first day of class. The index card allowed them to share this information privately. Thus, the first time I *verbally* took attendance in class, I was assured that I was respecting all of my students' names and identities. On one of those index cards a student identified himself as transgender and thanked me for asking for pronouns and preferred names. I believe it was my doing so that led to this student feeling comfortable enough to open up to me early on in the semester about his housing troubles.

Some background he shared with me later is as follows. While a traditionally aged student (between the ages of 18 and 22 when in my class), he had previously attended a four-year institution and left due to issues surrounding gender identity and lack of familial support. He is also a first-generation college student and supporting himself financially, so a community college seemed to be the right choice. He was living with his partner, had changed his name legally to his preferred name, was taking hormones to transition, and was taking honors classes. Everything seemed to be going well. Then his partner decided to leave him for someone else and kicked him—and his emotional support dog—out of their home.

At the beginning of the semester this student's performance was excellent. Honestly, his first paper in my introductory level course was one of the best I have read in almost 20 years of teaching. Suddenly, though, his attendance became sporadic. He was doing the work, but was rarely in class. When he was, he seemed distracted and upset. He left the classroom often and for long periods of time. Shortly before midterm, I called him into the hall just to ask how he was doing. He shared with me that he was currently living out of his car with his dog (a large breed that many might find "scary"), and that he was having a difficult time finding housing. He was concerned about finding a roommate(s) who would accept his gender identity but also finding housing that would allow him to keep his dog. Although Maryland Senate Bill 212, the Fairness for All Marylanders Act of 2014, states that a person cannot be denied housing based on gender identity (Maryland SB212, n.d.), it still happens. Additionally, just because a transgender person finds housing, it does not necessarily mean they will be safe. In fact, they deal with "[v]iolence and discrimination ... of pandemic proportions" (Catalano & Shlasko, 2013, p. 425). According to the United States Office for Victims of Crime (2014), "[o]ne in two transgender individuals are sexually abused or assaulted at some point in their lives. Some reports estimate that transgender survivors may experience rates of sexual assault up to 66 percent, often coupled with physical assaults or abuse." Also, in Maryland, service animals are protected under the federal Americans with Disabilities Act and state law, but emotional support animals are not (Guerin, n.d.).

As such, my student found himself essentially homeless and searching for a permanent, safe, and welcoming place to live. At the same time, my former administrative assistant and his friend (both honors students at the college) were looking for another roommate. I suggested that my student contact them, knowing that they would be accepting of his gender identity and that the atmosphere in the apartment would be one of intellectual rigor and emotional support. I also had been concerned that their current roommate (not a student) was distracting them from their studies as he had visitors at all hours and did not seem to need to work to support himself, while they are both international students and needed several jobs—in addition to being full-time students—in order to pay their bills. I normally do not involve myself with the personal lives of my students, but this was a special case. All of the students involved are conscientious, hard-working, and driven. They also are all individuals who society would label as "other" based on their race, religion, and/or gender.

Ultimately, my student did not end up living with those students because he found a place more conveniently located to campus. However, he was forced to have his parents take his dog because the housing accommodations would not allow an emotional support animal. Not surprisingly, this was an incredible loss in his life and his psychological issues intensified. The absences began again, and he called me one day and said that he was going to have to drop my class. I managed to talk him out of it and made it very clear that I would support him in his decision to get help at a psychological facility, but that I would not allow him to drop the class. We talked about the options and I encouraged him to take an Incomplete in the class which would allow him to complete his remaining assignments upon his return when he was mentally healthy and able to do the work to the best of his ability.

When I finally heard from him again, he was in a much better place emotionally and physically. He found a place to live that allowed him to have his dog with him, and he was ready to finish my class. The final assignment he had to complete was a research paper on a societal problem, and I encouraged him to write on the current service animal law in Maryland. The resultant paper was not only excellently written and argued, but he told me that he was able to find some legal support to help him if he finds himself in another problematic housing situation in the future. I felt that tying his life concerns in with the coursework was an excellent way for me to help him, not just as an educator but also as a person who cares about him, his mental health, his safety, and his academic success.

TAKEAWAYS

- Basic needs, including regular access to nourishing food, secure housing, and healthcare, are essentials that must be in place before a student can effectively prioritize academics or work. The inability to meet basic needs can create significant hardship and stress. Although basic needs are important to all students, they can become especially relevant to a student who is in distress.

- Oftentimes, relocation from a student's usual housing arrangements may be necessary. Faculty should know which departments on campus (and which administrators) can assist when students need emergency alternative housing arrangements on a temporary basis.

- This narrative illustrates an individual who has faced many transitions in a relatively short amount of time. It is important to assess the individual's current presentation of symptoms within a larger context. That is, consider how his surgery, threats to housing, and betrayal by a former partner all converge. Students do not exist in a vacuum.

- This narrative is also a good example of how students often do not need "rescuing;" that is, they do not need faculty to do things for them. They need support, encouragement, and/or suggestions. In this case the student was able to solve their problems in time. Providing empathy and support without doing the work for the student allows the student to experience resiliency and competency.

- The actions of the faculty member at the start of the semester went a long way to provide students with a level of safety. Many in education would argue that optimal learning can only occur when a student feels safe in the classroom. Relationships are foundational to the educational process.

QUESTIONS FOR REFLECTION

1. Break-ups, particularly those that involve infidelity, can impact both partners—but especially the one who feels betrayed. As is the case with other forms of trauma, those involved may experience cognitive, emotional, physiological, and spiritual symptoms that look like mania or depression. How would you go about determining whether or not key signs of any of these manifestations are present? How would you follow up with the student if you observe any of these signs?

2. Faculty, particularly those who genuinely care about their students, often feel the need to "rescue" students who are experiencing

distress. What challenges might you have to resist in rescuing a student? For example, it can be tempting to want to loan money to a student who is struggling financially, but loaning a student money can have unanticipated consequences as opposed to helping a student locate other sources of financial support. Would you ever consider loaning a student money in an emergency situation? Why or why not?

3. Most situations involving students who are experiencing distress have both a remedial component (dealing with the immediate circumstances) and a more preventative component (making sure the likelihood of them being back in a similar situation is minimal). In this narrative, what are some concrete actions that should have been taken in the short term to deal with the situation as it was unfolding? What are some concrete actions that need to be implemented in the long term to make sure the student does not find themselves in the same place in the future?

4. We can all become very invested in someone's life, especially if they are struggling. Sometimes we can become overly invested and need to take a step back. What limits and "indicators" do you have to know when you have become overly invested and need to take a step back? What are those "indicators" and limits and some potential options when you experience these indicators?

REFERENCES

Acker, J. (1990, June). Hierarchies, jobs, bodies: A theory of gendered organizations. *Gender and Society, 4*(2), 139–158.

Catalano, C., & Shlasko, D. (2013). Transgender oppression introduction. In M. Adams, W. J. Blumenfeld, H. W. Hackman, M. L. Peters, & X. Zuniga (Eds), *Readings for diversity and social justice* (3rd ed., pp. 425–431). New York, NY: Routledge.

Guerin, L. (n.d.). Maryland laws on service dogs and emotional support animals. Retrieved from www.nolo.com/legal-encyclopedia/maryland-laws-on-service-dogs-and-emotional-support-animals.html.

Maryland SB212. (n.d.) Retrieved from https://trackbill.com/bill/maryland-senate-bill-212-fairness-for-all-marylanders-act-of-2014/630633 (accessed September 29, 2019).

Office for Victims of Crime. (2014, June). *Responding to transgender victims of sexual assault.* Retrieved from www.ovc.gov/pubs/forge/sexual_numbers.html.

Ryle, R. (2018). *Questioning gender: A sociological approach* (3rd ed.). Thousand Oaks, CA: Sage.

Chapter Thirteen

Group Distress and Healing When Teaching Distressed Communities

Sylvia Mendoza Aviña

In the summer of 2016, I accepted a position in Chicana/o Studies at a community college in Southern California. The community college was 24% Latinx at the time, and the Chicana/o Studies courses were almost entirely Mexican/Chicanx[1] and included Central American and Haitian students. My first semester at this community college aligned with the 2016 presidential election, and the news media was filled with soundbites and direct quotes steeped in white supremacy, xenophobia, and anti-immigrant hate.

There was a sense of urgency teaching in Chicana/o Studies in this historical moment and in this specific region. Students sometimes expressed feelings of fear and uncertainty in our classroom discussions, especially during lectures centered on citizenship and immigration. While I have been a scholar of Gloria Anzaldúa's (1999) borderlands theory for the entirety of my academic career, I had yet to teach in a literal geopolitical borderland. Given the community college's proximity to the U.S.–Mexico border, many of the students were from mixed-status[2] families and/or undocumented themselves. As such, the conversations we had in the Chicana/o Studies classes about race, gender, class, sexuality, citizenship status and borders were not only interesting to the students, but relevant and urgent given the potential that existed for a white supremacist to win the presidency.

One of my challenges as a social justice educator then was to co-create a borderlands pedagogical praxis (Elenes, 2001, 2010) with the community college students that fostered a learning environment that centered the students and their experiences living in a borderland. Further, I was challenged to do this as a fourth-generation Tejana/Chicana who has had the privilege of citizenship for multiple generations and thus did not share the experiences of some of my students from mixed status and undocumented families. I had to (and continue to) push myself to learn to teach in a way that centered the experiences of the students living and attending college in borderlands spaces, recognizing our shared but also divergent experiences and material realities.

Chicana feminist educational researcher Alejandra Elenes (2001), drawing from Gloria Anzaldúa, defines border pedagogies as teaching practices that are committed to the

> elimination of racial, gender, class, and sexual orientation hierarchies by decentralizing hegemonic practices that places at the center of cultural practices a homogeneous belief in US society that has marginalized the cultural practices of people of color, women, and gays and lesbians.
>
> (pp. 689)

Border pedagogies are central to the field of Chicana/o Studies. To teach in the field of Chicana/o Studies is to understand that Chicanas/os are producers of knowledge through their cultural practices, languages, traditions, spiritualities, sexualities, bodies, and everyday experiences (Delgado Bernal, 2001; Delgado Bernal, Elenes, Godinez, & Villenas, 2006; Elenes, 2001, 2010). Border pedagogies then are an important part of the academic field of Chicana/o Studies and function to not only identify structures of oppression and develop approaches to dismantling all forms of oppression, but to also engage in teaching and learning with students holistically. This means recognizing that students teach and learn through their entire bodies, minds, and spirits (Lara, 2002)—that education occurs in their families, in their cultural practices and traditions, in their bodies, spiritualities, home spaces, and through relationship with the land (Delgado Bernal et al., 2006).

Incorporating border pedagogies into Chicana/o Studies courses then is central to the academic discipline and also a necessary praxis for Chicanx/Afro/Latinx students as a whole, as these pedagogies recognize the ways that these communities engage in knowledge production via sites not valued by traditional educational research (Elenes, 2001; Delgado Bernal et al., 2006; Delgado Bernal, 2001; Mendoza Aviña & Morales, 2018; Mendoza Aviña, 2016; Morales, Mendoza Aviña, & Delgado Bernal, 2016; Mendoza Aviña & Morales, in press). Further, border pedagogies are especially useful for Chicanx/Afro/Latinx[3] students during times of overt white supremacy, such as election years, given that these practices center the realities, histories, and experiences of communities thriving and surviving in literal geopolitical and metaphorical borderland spaces. In this way, border pedagogies serve as an approach to working not only with distressed students, but entire distressed communities during periods of heightened white supremacy and xenophobia.

During this particular semester and especially in conversations related to current events, students would sometimes withdraw from conversation, remaining quiet, but actively listening. Some students had increased absences throughout the semester. Some students expressed anger, especially after the election, sharing that they felt that dominant culture did not care about migrants and Black and Brown communities. Some students shared the strategies they and their families had developed given their undocumented status, to include informing each other via Facebook of ICE checkpoints throughout Southern California; sometimes even parking miles ahead of a checkpoint to wave down drivers to let them know ICE was ahead.

Students asked to listen to and watch certain music videos collectively in class, such as YG and Nipsey Hussle's "FDT"[4] and Molotov's "Frijolero,"[5] or would want to watch YouTube videos together, that they circulated on their social media platforms, of undocumented folks defending their humanity and right to work and exist. Other students would send emails outside of class, asking for resources for themselves and/or their families. In one instance, a student reached out to me to supply a letter on behalf of another student who was being held at a detention center nearby. I recognized then that I would need to save a draft of this letter to have on file for the future and needed to familiarize myself with local immigration lawyers and organizations to share with students.

Fortunately, many faculty and staff at the community college were aware of the realities of the undocumented/DACA student population on campus and created a task force that met regularly to provide services for the students. This included connecting with local immigration lawyers that were trustworthy and reputable and could provide counsel to students. The task force hoped the community college district would eventually hire its own immigration attorney for students to access at low cost. The task force also developed a resource page for the community college's website and to distribute to students that listed places for students to apply for/renew their DACA, seek legal counsel, and to connect with local organizations that centered on immigration, as well as provided resources such as food and clothing.

Building on this institutional support and the recognition that it is the responsibility of educators with privilege and access to connect students to community resources as a part of ensuring their academic achievement, I used my Chicana/o Studies classes as a space to organize workshops and information sessions. Guest lecturers during my time at the community college included Lead Organizer for ACLU's San Diego/Imperial Counties

Graciela Uriarte, who conducted a know your rights workshop about ICE raids with the students. Even if students did not immediately or directly need this information or these services, they were made aware of the fact that these organizations and community workers exist to work on behalf of the community. This became an important praxis given that students shared—particularly after lectures that focused heavily on colonialism and oppression—that structural change seemed impossible. They wondered what realistically could be done to effect change.

Because of this feedback, I began to refocus my lectures around resistance movements in the U.S. led by mothers, women, families, youth, and recognized the importance of highlighting the activism and labor of community organizers. One of our guest lecturers that academic school year was Laura Zavala, Director of Policy and Campaign Development with InnerCity Struggle, an organization known for its activism and organizing around public education in East Los Angeles. Zavala's presentation revealed how campaign organizers identify key players at the city and state level to push forward policy created by the community, such as challenging the school district's zero tolerance policies; creating and enacting policy that requires college preparatory courses be made available to all Los Angeles Unified School District Students; and securing funding to create wellness centers that provide healthcare services to students attending school in Los Angeles' East Side. Through the incorporation of these guest speakers, the students were made aware of the fact that resistance to oppression always exists and that communities have historically and will continue to organize on their own behalf. Further, the guest lecturers provided tangible examples of how to create structural change, on the ground through protests, but also through creating policy and holding local politicians accountable to serving their constituencies.

It was (and remains) an intense historical moment for Chicana/o Studies and Ethnic Studies students and educators. For educators, I feel it is our responsibility to incorporate current events into our praxis, accounting for the ways in which current policy and dominant discourses impact our students, their families, and the local community, and how this impacts their learning. This involves gauging the energy and mental health of our students in the classroom. I was mindful and aware of the necessity of reading the room each lecture to gauge what the students might need on any given day: would a traditional lecture suffice? Would the students need an in-class activity centered on art to invite a process of healing and meditation rather than a lecture? Did it seem like they were needing connections to community organizations and resources that a guest lecture could provide? Were the students aware of campus and local resources available to them and how could I ensure they had better access to this information? Did something

127

happen in the news media that I would need to address at the start of class, or account for in creating my lesson plan? If lecturing, was the content too intense, or too top down about structural oppression, and should I instead switch the lecture to focus on resistance, or the cultural contributions of Afro/Latinx communities? Did the students need a break from the content entirely, and should we schedule a library resource day to learn academic research skills instead? Teaching distressed communities terrorized by heightened white supremacy during an election year required tapping into border pedagogies that, in addition to preparing students academically in higher education, accounted for current events and placed an emphasis on mental health and healing from the realities of living in a borderlands.

TAKEAWAYS

- This is an excellent example of how a challenge or crisis could involve a large group of students instead of a single student coming to a faculty member for help. This example shows how faculty can respond at a systemic or community level, providing support and advice on a larger scale to a classroom. Nevitt Sandford once said something like, if you are going to challenge students, then you need to also support them.

- Issues related to culture, cultural and individual identities, and the intersection of societal and political circumstances, especially when related to generational and hegemonic beliefs, can be sensitive topics and can cause some discomfort for some students. Although faculty do not necessarily aim to create or expect distress for students in the classroom, there are times students will experience crisis through the topics discussed, microaggressions experienced, or interactions with peers or faculty.

- The key to working with students in these situations is being comfortable with being engaged in those conversations while trying to remain calm. In addition, even if the faculty member does not have similar lived experiences as those of the distressed student, they should try to validate and support the feelings, in a nonjudgmental manner, of those who have been targeted or triggered in the classroom. It is possible that just a few minutes of effective, active listening may be enough to help students feel cared about by their faculty member.

- This type of engagement can be difficult for a faculty member, especially if they are uncomfortable with conflict or defensive and staunch in their beliefs about the presenting or a related issue. Therefore, it is good for the faculty member to identify their "hot buttons" and level of comfort with conflict resolution. It is also good for a faculty member to identify challenges or problems (or potential problems) that are explicit and immediately evident in the classroom.

■   There can oftentimes exist a duality of supporting students in distress while also engaging other students in teachable moments. When "hot moments" occur in the classroom, in addition to supporting students experiencing distress, it is also important to engage thoughtfully and purposively in strategies that maintain a supportive climate with effective communication. Managing such moments can be a complex endeavor, but ultimately, faculty can play a significant role.

QUESTIONS FOR REFLECTION

1.   Faculty are not required or expected to be advocates, but some faculty are comfortable taking on the role of advocate. What are your feelings about this? If you are an advocate for a group of students, how might that impact your teaching, your role on campus, or your personal life?

2.   What does this narrative tell us about how classroom policy and students' attitudes and actions that reflect something deeper than surface-level biases and inequities can impact the classroom environment as well as their peers?

3.   What is your level of comfort with discussing sociopolitical issues that have seeped into the classroom as well as impacted the students you teach?

4.   At some point, faculty members should expect their students to enter crisis. What are some strategies you can have in place to prepare yourself for difficult conversations inside and outside of the classroom?

NOTES

1. Chicanx refers to those born in the U.S. of Mexican descent. The "x" at the end of Chicanx replaces the Spanish language masculine and feminine "a" and "o" to be inclusive of all gender identities and forms of expression. Latinx refers to those born in the U.S. with ties to Latin American countries.

2. Mixed status refers to citizenship status within the family, meaning some students might have citizenship, but their parents/grandparents/extended family members may be undocumented.

3. I use Chicanx/Afro/Latinx to refer to Latinx students across the diaspora that recognizes AfroLatinx communities that have been erased by a project of pan-Latinidad. For more on this, read Alan Pelaez Lopez's article, The X in Latinx is

129

a Wound, Not a Trend, http://efniks.com/the-deep-dive-pages/2018/9/11/the-x-in-latinx-is-a-wound-not-a-trend.
4. A hip hop anthem that denounced 45 and called for collaborative action between gangs and Black and Brown communities against white supremacy.
5. Frijolero translates to beaner, a racist slur used historically in the Southwest by racists to refer to Mexican/Chicanx communities.

REFERENCES

Anzaldúa, G. (1999). *Borderlands/la frontera: The new Mestiza*. San Francisco, CA: Aunt Lute Press.

Delgado Bernal, D. (2001). Learning and living pedagogies of the home: The Mestiza consciousness of Chicana students. *International Journal of Qualitative Studies in Education, 14*(5), 623–639.

Delgado Bernal, D., Elenes, C. A., Godinez, F. E., & Villenas, S. (Eds.). (2006). *Chicana/Latina education in everyday life: Feminista perspectives on pedagogy and epistemology*. Albany, NY: State University of New York Press.

Elenes, A. (2001). Trasformando fronteras: Chicana feminist transformative pedagogies. *International Journal of Qualitative Studies in Education, 14*(5), 689–702.

Elenes, A. (2010). *Transforming borders: Chicana/o popular culture and pedagogy*. United Kingdom: Lexington Books.

Lara, I. (2002). Healing sueños for academia. In G. E. Anzaldua, & A. Keating (Eds.), *This bridgewe call home* (pp. 433–438). New York, NY: Routledge.

Mendoza Aviña, S. (2016). "That's ratchet": A Chicana feminist Rasquache pedagogy as entryway to understanding the material realities of contemporary Latinx elementary aged youth. *Equity & Excellence in Education, 49*(4), 468–479.

Mendoza Aviña, S., & Morales, S., (2018). "Ratchet of the earth": Using Black and Chicana feminisms to understand how brown youth resist in schools. *Chicana/Latina Studies: The Journal of Mujeres Activas en Letras y Cambio Social (MALCS)*.

Mendoza, S., & Morales, S. (in press). EntreMundos: Extending Anzaldúa's Borderlands to Latina/o elementary youth. In A. I. Fukushima, R. González, L. Maparyan, A. Revilla, & M. Richardson (Eds.), *Saving Our Own Lives: Queer, Indigenous, Muxerista, Womanist, and Feminist of Color Voices*. San Antonio, Texas: Third Woman Press.

Morales, S., Mendoza, S., & Delgado Bernal, D. (2016). Education in nepantla: A Chicana feminist approach to engaging Latina/o elementary youth in ethnic studies. In T. L. Buenavista, J. R. Marin, A. J. Ratcliff, & D. M. Sandoval (Eds.), *White washing American education: The new culture wars in ethnic studies*, (pp. 67–93). Santa Barbara, California: Prager Publishers.

About the Editors

Monica Galloway Burke is a Professor in the Department of Counseling and Student Affairs at Western Kentucky University. Prior to her 22 years of experience as a faculty member and practitioner in Student Affairs and Higher Education, she worked in the field of mental health. Dr. Burke has authored numerous peer-reviewed articles in scholarly journals and contributed chapters to various books. She also served as the lead author for *Helping Skills for Working with College Students: Applying Counseling Theory to Student Affairs Practice* (Routledge, 2017) and as co-editor for *No Ways Tired: The Journey for Professionals of Color in Student Affairs*, a three-volume set (Information Publishing, 2019). Additionally, she has conducted numerous workshops and presentations at the international, national, regional, state, and local levels. Dr. Burke currently serves and has served on editorial boards of professional journals as a co-editor, associate editor, and reviewer. She also supervised numerous research theses, dissertations, and research projects, some of which led to co-authored published manuscripts with students.

Karl Laves is the Associate Director and Clinical Care Coordinator at the Western Kentucky University Counseling Center. He has taught in the psychology, counseling, and student affairs, and psychological sciences departments. He is a licensed counseling psychologist and received his doctoral degree from the University of Missouri-Columbia. He has provided supervision to graduate students and counseling center staff and frequently presents at counseling center staff conferences.

Jill Duba Sauerheber is a Professor and Department Head of the Department of Counseling and Student Affairs at Western Kentucky University. She has published over 40 peer-reviewed journal articles and three books, as well as conducted over 60 scholarly international, national, and regional presentations. She is the past-president of the North American Society of Adlerian Psychology, and has served on various editorial boards of professional journals. She is a graduate of the 2014 Harvard Graduate School of Education Management Development Program which focused on leadership development in higher education. Dr. Sauerheber maintains a part-time counseling practice in which she specializes in trauma and couples counseling; she is Eye Movement Desensitization and Reprocessing (EMDR) certified and trained in Somatic Experiencing, Brainspotting and Gottman Couples Therapy Method.

Aaron W. Hughey is a University Distinguished Professor and Program Coordinator in the Department of Counseling and Student Affairs at Western Kentucky University, where he oversees the Master's degree program in Student Affairs in Higher Education as well as graduate certificate programs in International Student Services and Career Services. Before joining the faculty in 1991, he spent years in progressive administrative positions, including five years as the Associate Director of University Housing at WKU. He was also Head of the Department of Counseling and Student Affairs for five years before returning to the faculty full-time in 2008. Dr. Hughey has degrees from the University of Tennessee at Martin (Secondary Education—Biological Science), the University of Tennessee at Knoxville (Educational Psychology), Western Kentucky University (Counselor Education—Student Personnel Services), and Northern Illinois University (Educational Administration with an Emphasis in Higher Education). He has authored (or co-authored) over 60 refereed publications on a wide range of issues including student learning and development, recruitment and retention, leadership, standardized testing, diversity, and educational administration. He regularly presents at national and international conferences and consults extensively with companies and schools. He also provides training programs and conducts webinars for multiple organizations on a variety of topics centered on evidence-based best practices.

132

About the Contributors

Colin Cannonier obtained a PhD in Economics at Louisiana State University and is currently an Associate Professor at Belmont University and a GLO Fellow. He began his career working as a country economist in the Eastern Caribbean. His research focus is in applied economics with emphasis in health, labor, and education and how they intersect with public policy and economic development. He has authored several peer-reviewed articles in scholarly journals such as *Economics of Education Review*, *Journal of Labor Research*, *Review of Economics of the Household*, and *Journal of Demographic Economics*. His research has also been featured in popular outlets such as the *Harvard Business Review* and the UNESCO. In addition, he has made numerous presentations at national, regional, and international forums such as the London School of Economics, the American Economic Association, Paris School of Economics, the European Economic Association, the NBER Summer Institute and central banks. In September 2019 he delivered the feature address at the Government of St. Kitts and Nevis Annual Prime Minister's Independence Lecture Series. Dr. Cannonier has had the honor of representing his native country in two sports: cricket and soccer.

Toya Conston is a Clinical Assistant Professor in the Human Development and Family Studies Program (HDFS) in the College of Education at the University of Houston. Dr. Conston's clinical interests include analyzing factors that lead to persistence and graduation of underrepresented students from four-year institutions. Her work also extends into the Third Ward Community where she implements a service-learning component "Ed Psych in Real Life" and Strong Men of Valor (SMOV). Both programs are geared towards Mentorship. Dr. Conston also serves as an adjunct faculty member at Texas Southern University in their graduate program, Educational Administration and Foundations Educational Administration and Foundations.

Ryan Donovan joined the faculty of the Department of Health and Exercise Science at Colorado State University where he currently serves as a Senior Teaching Instructor and the Director of Undergraduate Advising after earning his Master's degree in 2007. In a department with more than 1,000 students, Ryan has the privilege of teaching and interacting with hundreds of students every semester. His courses range from first-year personal health and wellness seminars to senior capstone experiences. Ryan's teaching and advising philosophy is to *educate and empower each student during every interaction*. Outside of teaching and advising, Ryan is an accomplished marathon runner who loves spending time outdoors with his wife, Rachel, and daughter, Clover.

Christopher L. Giroir is an experienced educator with a demonstrated history of working in the field of higher education at both public and private institutions. He began his career in higher education by working in student affairs, in particular residence life and housing. After working for several years with residence life, he transitioned into other areas on the university campus, including campus activities, intramurals/recreation, campus welcome center, Greek Life, student leadership, and orientation/FYE. Dr. Giroir brings his years of practical work experience into the classroom as he enjoys working to prepare the next generation of university administrators. Currently working as an Associate Professor in Educational Leadership (Higher Education Administration) at the University of Louisiana at Lafayette, he is working with graduate students pursuing their EdD degree. He has served in graduate faculty roles at both The University of Southern Mississippi and Arkansas Tech University. In addition to faculty roles held, he also held administrative duties in higher education that included serving as graduate program coordinator, department head, and an associate dean for a graduate college.

Lia Howard is the Executive Director of the Philadelphia Commons Institute and an Assistant Professor of Political Science and Liberal Studies in the Templeton Honors College at Eastern University. Prior to the Philadelphia Commons Institute, she taught American Politics in the Political Science Department at Saint Joseph's University. Dr. Howard was a Critical Writing Fellow and taught in the Political Science Department at the University of Pennsylvania. She is a Non-Resident Senior Fellow at the Program for Research on Religion and Urban Civil Society (PRUCCS) and also a Senior Fellow at the Robert A. Fox Leadership Program, both at the University of Pennsylvania. She is also a Non-Resident Scholar at Baylor University's Institute for Studies of Religion (ISR). Dr. Howard studied English and French as an undergraduate at the University of Pennsylvania.

134

She received her MA and PhD in Political Science also from the University of Pennsylvania. She lives in the Philadelphia area with her husband and their three daughters.

Trish Lindsey Jaggers is an Assistant Professor in the Department of English at Western Kentucky University. She is the author of *De-Composition: Rigor Mortis* and *Holonym: A Collection of Poems*, is an award-winning Kentucky poet and Assistant Professor in WKU's Department of English where she teaches composition, literature, creative writing, and poetry, and mentors a flock of students and writers.

Leigh Johnson-Migalski is an Associate Professor in the Department of Psychology at Adler University. She has a Diplomate in Adlerian Psychology. She is a licensed clinical psychologist who has worked for years in medical centers, community mental health, and group and individual practice with clients across the life span. She also does parent education. She has over ten publications and has presented numerous times in the field.

Theresia Johnson-Ratliff is Director of Field Education for the Master of Social Work in the School of Social Work at Jackson State University in Jackson, Mississippi. She has a Master of Arts degree in Grief Counseling, a Master of Social Work, and a PhD in Urban Higher Education. Her research interests are adult learners, gerontology, health and mental health. Dr. Ratliff is a Licensed Clinical Social Worker for the State of Mississippi where she has a private practice.

Andrea Kirk-Jenkins is an Assistant Professor in the Department of Counseling and Student Affairs at Western Kentucky University. She currently serves as the Clinical Mental Health program coordinator as well as the coordinator for the Addictions Certificate. Her research interests include eating disorders, college student population, addictions, crisis counseling, supervision, and professional development. Her clinical passion lies within crisis counseling, particularly sexual assault, interpersonal violence, suicidal and homicidal ideation. Dr. Kirk-Jenkins feels passionate about assisting in developing competent and passionate counselors, as well as supporting students' research endeavors as she is currently serving on multiple dissertation and thesis committees.

Sylvia Mendoza Aviña is a lecturer at the University of Texas at San Antonio in the department of Bicultural-Bilingual Studies. Her research interests include Chicanx/Latinx feminisms in education, Anzaldúan borderlands theory, and Chicanx/Ethnic Studies in K-12 schools. Dr. Mendoza Aviña is currently a co-editor of a forthcoming special issue in *Urban Education* focusing on transformational resistance related to students of color. She received her PhD from the University of Utah, in the department of Education, Culture and Society.

Megan X. Schutte is an Associate Professor of English and the Director of the Writing and Literacy Centers at the Community College of Baltimore County. She is also a doctoral candidate in the Higher Education Administration program at Morgan State University. When she has time to be a normal human, she loves to travel and watch soccer (often together), design her own shoes, and play with her nephews.

Index

Taylor & Francis Group
an **informa** business

Taylor & Francis eBooks

www.taylorfrancis.com

A single destination for eBooks from Taylor & Francis
with increased functionality and an improved user
experience to meet the needs of our customers.

90,000+ eBooks of award-winning academic content in
Humanities, Social Science, Science, Technology, Engineering,
and Medical written by a global network of editors and authors.

TAYLOR & FRANCIS EBOOKS OFFERS:

A streamlined
experience for
our library
customers

A single point
of discovery
for all of our
eBook content

Improved
search and
discovery of
content at both
book and
chapter level

REQUEST A FREE TRIAL
support@taylorfrancis.com

 Routledge
Taylor & Francis Group

 CRC Press
Taylor & Francis Group

Made in the USA
Monee, IL
04 May 2021

67718030R00083